INTENTIONAL Integrity

GARNETT REID

TEN LIFE STRATEGIES FOR WHOLENESS FROM THE BOOK OF JOB

randall house
114 Bush Rd | Nashville, TN 37217 | randallhouse.com

Published by Randall House Publications
114 Bush Road
Nashville, TN 37217

ISBN 9780892656356

Printed in the United States of America

בֵּן חָכָם יְשַׂמַּח־אָב

Proverbs 10:1a

To our sons Hugh and Seth, men of integrity,
who make their father glad.

TABLE OF CONTENTS

PREFACE

Doctrine and life, colours and light, in one
When they combine and mingle, bring
A strong regard and awe . . . .
—George Herbert, *"The Windows"*

You know, the one with all the well meaning rules
that don't work out in real life, uh, Christianity.
—Homer Simpson, *The Simpsons*

"Reality TV"—sure, my real world includes racing around the world to win a million dollars. And Donald Trump tells me all the time, "You're fired!" Most every few weeks I form "alliances" on remote tropical islands trying to win that million, too. It happens to me all the time. No, the truth is that most of these "reality" shows are just downright unreal for most of us.

They do, however, raise an issue that for most Christians is at the heart of life itself: taking our faith with us from the sanctuary to the real world, or being sure that what we believe shapes how we behave. A friend said it well at a small group prayer meeting when he petitioned, "Lord, O that I would be what I seem to be, and that I would seem to be what I really am." We may sing hymns, study Scripture, and offer prayers on Sunday, but do these "church drills" make any difference in our thinking and living in the sales meeting Monday morning or at the shop when we have to work overtime? Do we live the truth no matter where we are or what life brings our way?

I suspect more of us have problems along these lines than we are willing to admit. I know I do. A *U. S. News and World Report* article addressed this concern from the perspective of society at large. Despite the fervor over popular books such as the *Left Behind* series, *The Prayer of Jabez*, and *The Purpose Driven Life*, as well as Mel Gibson's cinematic blockbuster *The Passion of the Christ*, "evangelicals . . . are acting more and more like the rest of us," claims Jeffrey L. Sheler. Instead of Christian believers influencing the culture, we are "far more shaped by the culture" than *vice versa*, Boston College professor Alan Wolfe contends.

While I am concerned about the broad culture of evangelical life, solutions begin with me and with you as individuals. It's the consistency, or lack of it, of how I live *my* faith and how my character impacts you that must serve as the point of origin for the renewal flame of Christian integrity. That's how I must begin—with my decisions, my heart, my life.

Not so long ago several moral failings plagued my circle of friends. With word of each new case of substandard Christian living, we grieved as if a loved one had died. Thankfully, some of those at fault have sought and achieved varying degrees of restoration. In the course of those difficult events, one friend voiced a question wrenched from the honesty of his broken heart: "Does Christianity work in real life anymore?"

Actually my friend's question was the wrong one. The issue is not whether biblical faith is able to shape our lives, but whether or not we will live our faith. Will we be Christians? Our real concern must be *integrity*. The word "integrity" refers to wholeness, to that which is complete, unmixed, undivided. An "integral" component of an electronic circuit is a part necessary to complete the circuit. Without that element there is no "integrity," no system. Integrity in life shows up in consistent character and completes the "circuit" of faith we profess.

The question remains, though, what kind of character do we display? What sort of consistent actions define our behavior? In one sense, someone may live a consistent life, but that consistency may reflect a commitment to the wrong principles, say, like a Hitler or a Charles Manson. Consistency alone, then, is not enough to produce a life of *Christian* integrity. Such a lifestyle also requires a bedrock commitment to truth—not just "a" truth or "truth" as I tailor it to suit my individual preferences, but the absolute, changeless truth of God's character as He reveals Himself in the Bible. When we bond our lives to truth, to the person of God in a living relationship with Him, the result is integrity. Integrity equals commitment plus truth.

An analogy of a building helps us see how these two components produce integrity. Architects and engineers speak of the "integrity" of a structure, meaning the assembly of standard materials in proportion and order based on a sound design. When these two essentials are present, the building safely stands. There is no danger of its collapse. Its integrity depends not only on the presence of all the proper materials—wood, concrete, steel, and all the rest—but also on the accuracy of the blueprint, the design. Are the engineering theories sound and the measurements correct? To be people of integrity, we need a "take-it-all, Lord" commitment of our lives (the materials) wedded to the builder's perfect truth (the design).

Integrity means living with a center, an axis, holding the person together. The axis is God and His truth, and the spokes which radiate from it are all the details of my life. He makes it cohere. A committed promise to be a person of integrity energizes every part of me: mind, heart, will, and body. My thinking must investigate the world of ideas, all the while submitting those ideas to the scrutiny of God's truth. The things that are true, noble, right, and excellent must shape the way I think. My heart must then feel deeply about what is true. I need to love the truth not only because it is right in and of itself, but also because it is the best thing for me.

Yet knowing and loving the right things are not enough. I have to exercise my will every day to do those things. Physically, with my body, I must conduct myself in a way that honors the center, the axis—God. "The final component of the . . . process for moral behavior [integrity] is for a person to have sufficient perseverance, ego strength, and implementation skills to be able to follow through on his or her intention to behave morally," says Christian psychologist Judy TenElshof.

The real test of integrity's worth in our lifestyle, however, comes when we persevere in living for God when it seems too tough to do that. Integrity withstands testing. This turn of suffering makes Job's integrity all the more compelling: it survives the ash heap! His adversity becomes his teacher, finally revealing Job as the small servant of God he is, his comforters as the pretenders they are, and *Shaddai* as the wise Redeemer who vindicates His glory.

So the book of Job comes to life in the storm. My personal experience with Job has navigated strong headwinds over the last decade-and-a-half. During that time, from my ash heap, though it hardly compares to Job's, I have witnessed my mother's arduous and ultimate struggle with terminal disease; my own chronic illness, dialysis, organ transplant and recovery; and our son's cancer diagnosis, surgery, and healing. Integrity means more to me than it ever has. To live a *true* life, a life inside-out for all, especially God, matters more than impressing people with an appearance disconnected from my heart. Regardless of what's happening around us and to us, the things that count most happen within us. These are realities we must tend first. They stay with us and as they deepen in the soil of our soul, we grow. This is the life of truth. This is integrity.

CHAPTER 1

A Promise Kept

. . . (L)et God know my integrity!
Oh, that I had the indictment written by my adversary!
I would bind it on me as a crown;
I would give him an account of all my steps . . . .
Job 31:6b, 35b, 36b, 37a

"The book [of Job] hinges on the issue of integrity. . . . [W]e watch for cracks in Job's own integrity as he loses, one by one, everything he values," Philip Yancey reminds us. Three times in the opening chapters we read this description of Job: he was "blameless and upright, one who feared God and turned away from evil." The Hebrew word translated "blameless" has the idea of something complete, something whole. Job's character lacked no essential quality. He was "upright"—literally, "straight"—the moral equivalent before God of what an exact perpendicular is to an engineer.

WHEREVER YOU THUMP

These qualities might lead us to think Job was perfect, that he might never have sinned. Such is not the case, though, as Job himself admits: "If I wash myself with snow and cleanse my hands with lye, yet you (God) will plunge me into a pit, and my own clothes will abhor me." Job came from Adam's stuff, depravity included. Still, this good man from Uz was a godly, righteous man. Following the enormous tragedies that had battered him, Job worshiped and blessed God's name. He had taught, encouraged, and supported those around him who needed help. Even Eliphaz, his accusing friend, said as much. The leading officials of his community had respected and honored Job for his selfless charity toward bereft townspeople. No doubt about it—if you were looking for a model of integrity in the east country, Job was your man.

At my grandfather's funeral, a longtime friend from a nearby farm said of him, "The thing about Tom Haun was that he was always the same. No matter where he was or whom he was with, you knew what kind of a man he was, what he believed. He was the same wherever you 'thumped' him," referring, I think, to the down-home practice of "thumping" a melon with your finger to judge its ripeness. I like to think that Job passed the "thumping" test with flying colors.

No matter how we examine Job's life, we keep coming back to the idea of integrity. That single descriptor says it all—Job was a man of integrity. The Lord says as much: "He still holds fast his integrity." Job's wife, even in her bitter outburst after losing her children, speaks of it. He himself resolves, "Till I die I will not put away my integrity from me."

TRUE EVEN IN THE DARK

When Job crosses their minds, many people think that his story is all about adversity—why do the righteous suffer? The theme of suffering is indeed a vital piece of the book's puzzle, but it is *not* the centerpiece. Instead, the broad storyline of Job involves God's freedom to be God, to act sovereignly, and the need for human beings to submit to God's free actions through constant, unwavering trust in Him. When will a person trust God? Will we "bless His name" when our circumstances would lead us to question His goodness and His justice? These are the inquiries Job must answer in his soul. This issue explains why Job, though not without sin, is innocent of the charges his friends level against him. He does not deserve what he is going through. As Francis Andersen discerns, "The book of Job loses its point if the righteousness of Job is not taken as genuine." Even as God tightens the screws and turns up the heat, Job will emerge from all of it unscathed. That's what we expect to happen.

In the end, God never answers the "why the righteous suffer" question. He doesn't have to answer it. Instead we're the ones who have to give *Him* an answer—the "yes" or "no" of our hearts, minds, and bodies surrendered to whatever He has planned for us. He gives us Himself; we give Him ourselves in return. My friend Tom McCullough captured this lesson for me in one line he wrote in an e-mail. As his sweet wife Patty endured intense pain during her final days of life, Tom's message spoke of trusting in a good God no matter what: "Help me not to question in the dark what I have known to be true in the light," he prayed.

Job's story of integrity in the face of relentless trials makes this book one of the most pivotal in the Bible. Here we find a man who is not a covenant Israelite, who likely lived before God's revelation to Moses, suffering as few have ever suffered. Yet he remains a God-fearer, a special object of God's love in the middle of Satan's attack. Only someone bolstered by a tenacious faith could display integrity under Job's circumstances. In his lifetime he never learns why he has lost everything, even though he hears directly from God and becomes a model corresponding to the ultimate innocent sufferer, the coming Christ.

LAST STAND

The author of the book is clearly a craftsman with words and tells Job's story with beauty and balance. We run the risk of misunderstanding the message of Old Testament writers if we are insensitive to how they express it. So it is with our reading of Job. How the book is put together contributes to what the author wants to emphasize. Picture a set of bookends enclosing several volumes and you have an overview of Job's structure. The bookends are the prologue and epilogue, both set in prose.

Between are the "books"—that is, the individual units of poetry: dialogue, monologues, and a hymn.

Another way to think of the layout is to view the book of Job as a football field. The prologue and epilogue are the end zones and in the center, chapter 28, is the wisdom hymn—the fifty-yard line. Moving from one goal line toward the middle of the field, we come to the three speech cycles involving Job, Eliphaz, Bildad, and Zophar. As we leave midfield and move toward the other goal line, we encounter Job's three monologues, Elihu's discourse, and the Lord's speeches. The touchdown comes when we reach the end zone—Job's restoration.

Just before we hear from Elihu and God Himself, the book reaches a critical point. Job speaks at length for the last time in chapters 29, 30, and 31 before his brief confessions in chapters 40 and 42. In chapter 29 he fondly recalls the past when he was "in his prime," enjoying his family and God's favor. People loved and respected him for his generous spirit, and he fully expected to live out his days "like a king among his troops." "But now," he begins in chapter 30, "they laugh at me." Job languishes as an outcast, "a brother of jackals" alone with his endless pain. His "prosperity has passed away like a cloud" and his skin blackens, pulling away from his body like dry bark from a tree. The reason for all these terrors is clear to Job, or so he thinks: "God has cast me into the mire . . . . [W]ith the might of your (God's) hand you persecute me." *Shaddai*—God Himself—has become Job's enemy for no apparent reason, and no help seems imminent.

So Job takes the stand in his own defense one last time. In chapter 31 he carefully unfolds a final summary of his case for integrity. Those who heard him would have been familiar with his strategy since apparently it mirrored a common legal maneuver in the ancient world. His oath is in keeping with the many terms and metaphors in the book reflecting the judicial system of his day. In some ways, reading Job is like looking over a second millennium B. C. script of *Law and Order*! For example, the text refers to guilt, innocence, and righteousness, to formal hearings, arguing cases, and a defense attorney ("mediator"). This tie-in with jurisprudence is no accident since Job was once involved in administering justice in his own town. Earlier in the book he sets the stage for this climactic defense with brief statements defending his innocence.

"MAY LIGHTNING STRIKE ME"

Chapter 31 is built around the template of a formal oath of innocence. The procedure went something like this. When a defendant faced charges of wrongdoing, he could call for a hearing in which his accuser had to present evidence against him. If no such evidence or witness appeared, the accused could issue a legally-binding "affidavit" declaring his innocence.

In essence, the defendant—Job in this case—calls upon God to punish him for his crimes if indeed he had committed them. Job publicly announces, "If I am guilty of" whatever the charge is, "then may God" impose a particular penalty on me, or "let me" suffer a specific punishment. Similar statements show up elsewhere in the Old Testament. In fact, we say much the same thing today when we declare, for example, "If I am lying, then may lightning strike me." Of course unlike Job, we mean this tongue-in-cheek, not as a serious imprecation. Even if we aren't telling the truth, we don't expect the clouds to suddenly roll in and thunder to boom.

Clearly the trajectory of Job's statement extends beyond his example of past integrity and reaches ahead to offer promise of the kind of man he intends to be in days to come. The oath thus forms the staging area for future displays of his honor and so becomes a vow or a promise as well. Our study of the chapter will more-or-less follow the order of its ten stanzas, with a couple of exceptions I will explain along the way. Though students of Job dispute the exact number of subjects he addresses, we will examine ten qualities of integrity he embraces as commitments:

Purity (verses 1-4)
Honesty (verses 5-6)

Contentment (verses 7–8 and 24–25)
Loyalty (verses 9–12)
Equity (verses 13–15)
Compassion (verses 16–23 and 31–32)
Worship (verses 26–28)
Forgiveness (verses 29–30)
Confession (verses 33–34)
Stewardship (verses 38–40)

In verses 35–37, Job "signs his name" to the pledge, sealing his testimony of innocence.

A TRIO OF CONCERNS

Each chapter of this book examines three critical issues. First, we walk through Job's words themselves. What is he saying? What did he mean when he made these statements? We must not bypass this initial step because the biblical text itself must guide us as we apply the principles in our setting. The second part of each chapter paints a representative picture of how that particular issue fares in today's culture. What in the world keeps us from lives of integrity? How do these virtues play at dinner parties, on VH-1, at the campus student center, on Twitter® and blog sites, in the office break room, on the big screen, or in the secular mind of that neighbor across the street we wave to each day?

The third segment of each chapter is the most urgent. What action do I need to take today to be a person of integrity? Given what I know of God's revealed truth, the culture I engage, and the unique person I am, what should my life look like? Integrity is not simply a lofty ideal to contemplate; it is a word plus an action strung together with more words and actions again and again to make a life, a true life, a whole life.

FOLLOWING THROUGH

The oath Job takes is simply a promise wrapped in words for

all to hear, including God. Please don't dismiss what he says as all hype—just words, with nothing to back them up or make them happen. Job's track record indicates otherwise. The commitments in this vow are not the flighty ideals of a dreamer; no, Job has forged them into his soul and has lived them all his life. We shouldn't doubt for a minute the momentum of his will merged with his fear of God to keep him moving along a well-marked path of integrity for the rest of his days.

The lives of God's elect in the Old Testament resonate with these promises. That's all an oath is: a promise or vow to God sealed with a formal statement. We shouldn't shy away from making commitments to God just because we sometimes don't keep them or because brothers and sisters we know fail to live up to the promises they've made. Most people who later break vows fully intend to keep them when they make them. Personal relationships always involve commitments.

Lewis Smedes reminds us of "The Power of Promises":

> Yes, somewhere people still make and still keep promises. They choose not to quit when the going gets rough because they promised to see it through. They stick to lost causes. They hold on to a love grown cold. They stay with people who have become a pain in the neck. They still dare to make promises and to keep the promises they make.

Psychologists testify of goal-setters who make resolutions and sustain them because they are committed to the difference fulfilled promises will make in their lives. They envision the change that will come with the vow, and that quest becomes motivation enough to take the small steps in the life of faith each day, no matter the cost, to keep the promise.

A reminder is in order, though, in our case, as well as in Job's, that we become people of consistent character not through the sheer grit and mettle of our will. God, who made us in His image and who always fulfills His promises, "works in us . . . to will and to work for his good pleasure." The beautiful work integrity brings to our lives exalts the skilled Potter, not the marred clay.

VINTAGE INTEGRITY

When we read these simple words of this ancient sufferer, I fear we don't really grasp the magnitude of what he's saying. Consider that unlike most of the other oaths of innocence in early civilizations, Job's vows deal almost exclusively with ethical principles, not with formal religious ritual. He's not talking about what will happen to him if he has botched some small detail in offering a sacrifice, or about what punishment might beset him in some shady afterlife after he's dead. Instead Job reflects on whether or not he has slept with another man's wife, or treated his workers fairly, or fed the hungry.

What's more, Job likely lived during the time of Abraham and Jacob—some two thousand years before Christ was born. Moses wouldn't be around to climb Mount Sinai for another five and one-half centuries. Not that it would have mattered to Job since he was almost certainly not an Israelite anyway. Uz, his homeland, was probably located in Edomite territory, near what is now the Syria-Arabia border. Think of it! *Job 31 provides us with one of the earliest profiles of what the fear of God looks like incarnate—a set of personal convictions not borrowed from some inherited tradition or imposed by some law code, but imbedded within a man's soul through his friendship with God.* Nothing in the ancient texts resembles what we read here.

Consider, too, that Job addresses not just what integrity *does*, what it looks like on the outside. He also probes the inner person, the motives of the will, the interior of the heart. Job stresses that his actions grow out of a consciousness grounded in godliness; how he lived in his world reflected what he believed in his heart. In some ways, Job's oath mirrors the concern for motive reflected in Jesus' Sermon on the Mount.

The church somehow has bought into the notion that the Old

Testament is only about the letter of the law and external compliance with the commandments, not about the heart. Job 31 alone blows away such an ill-informed caricature. Lust, covetousness, heart affection, hidden sin—though others never see these struggles of the spirit, these matters entrusted to the heart, Job knows better than to leave them out of his game plan for integrity.

This oath essentially integrates Job's private life with his public one. They were not two different arenas for him, nor should they be for us. The disciplines of his spirit and the strength of his will as a man who feared God shaped his entire persona, and he was not ashamed for people to know that. An essential oneness linked Job's character with God's. Sure, to us Job wouldn't have looked very "cool," covered with sores, sitting there alone on the ash pile. Yet he had nothing to hide. He knew firsthand wholeness and holiness in the deepest levels of his consciousness. Had he not known them, Job's words would be irrelevant, hypocritical, and even ludicrous. His claims would be nothing more than an empty wind sweeping over a field of chaff, a life not of wheat and barley but of thorns and briers.

"Bring your warrant against me," Job invites the adversary. "Go ahead—file charges! Serve the papers! You'll see nothing written on them. In fact," he revels, "I would gladly turn them into a crown I'd wear so no one will doubt that I have lived with integrity."

Without integrity's crown,

lust explodes purity;

lies haunt our pretense of truth;

anything goes for a price;

suspicion plagues a marriage;

cruelty brutalizes human weakness;

the blessed ignore those in need of blessing;

everything that is not God becomes god;

love becomes a sullen, grisly tyrant;
neighbors retreat into self;
we all hide behind propriety's door;
the people He made shove God off the planet;
stinkweed grows wild;
and flames burn to ashes integrity's crown.

The Purity Promise:

Job Resolves to Avoid Lust

Job 31:1–4

I have made a covenant with my eyes;
how then could I gaze at a virgin?
What would be my portion from God above
and my heritage from the Almighty on high?
Is not calamity for the unrighteous,
and disaster for the workers of iniquity?
Does not he see my ways
and number all my steps?

Ironically the author of the book *Lust* in a series on the Seven Deadly Sins doesn't really consider lust a sin. In fact, Simon Blackburn sees his calling in the work to "rescue [lust] from the echoing denunciations of old men of the deserts" such as Job, whom I assume he would class with these antique curmudgeons. Blackburn's thesis fits well in our culture's mindset where the biggest concern about sexual passion is that we not repress whatever appetites and urges may please us. Freedom to lust, to seduce, to gratify—these comprise a 21st century "bill of erotic rights."

For Christ's people, however, the issue of lust often meets us first not as adults in seedy bookstores, strip clubs, or adult satellite channels, but as teenagers curious about the scantily-clad *Cosmo* or *Vogue* model on the magazine's glossy cover, or the *Playboy* collection in our friend's closet, or the roving hands of our date on prom night. Christians must respond decisively to control these early encounters with impure desires then maintain deployment against this powerful intruder that will dog our steps throughout life.

In some ways, Job's first resolution startles us. Lust? Why begin here? Some preamble extolling *Shaddai* or another less sensitive, "in-polite-company" subject might seem more proper as an opening. But this is where the battle rages in life—in the dark corners of our minds that harbor the most dearly-held fugitives on the run from the light of God's truth and from the dominion of His sovereignty. Winning this battle constitutes a preemptive strike against that cherished, entrenched stronghold of self we love to guard at all costs. When the fortress of our concealed desires held in defiance of the Master's command falls, word spreads quickly that all of the other outposts of resistance must yield to Him as well.

WHAT JOB SAYS: THE LOOK OF LUST

Job commits himself to avoid any thought that might stimulate him to illicit desire. "I have made a covenant with my eyes," he declares, to stay away from longing stares at young women. Here he uses the language of formal pacts common in his culture. A "covenant" is a pledged agreement making a promise and assuming the obligation to keep that trust. It's as if Job and his eyes have worked out a deal regarding what they will allow or refuse entry into his mind.

What appeals to our eyes creates a desire in our hearts, as Job recognizes. In light of this committed promise, his question, "How then could I gaze at a young woman?" assumes an answer on the order of, "Of course, I could not. I have resolved within myself that I will not." Job refuses to give in to the excuse heard so often: "It just happened. I couldn't help it." He could help it because he had willed to control himself.

The word translated "gaze at" suggests carefully considering a thing, as seen in its use elsewhere in the book. Job realizes that the longer we contemplate how attractive and pleasurable an experience might be, the more inclined we are to do whatever it takes to make that fantasy become real. "Then desire when it has conceived gives birth to sin," James affirms. So this man of integrity will avoid ogling women, refusing by deliberate discipline to "feast his eyes" on what appeals to those ugly ragings on the dark side of his nature.

DESERVED DISASTER

If Job were guilty of improper sexual thoughts, he knows that ruin would follow. God would allot him a "portion" and an "inheritance" due his crime. Should he lust for a woman, he would get what he deserves. The shattering assault of God's judgment would bring "calamity" and "disaster," two terms suggesting the fierce consequences overtaking the unrighteous. Assuming his guilt were real, Job goes so far as to class himself among those who work iniquity, those who elsewhere fall under the category of those who "do not know God."

The irony of Job's situation, though, lies in the fact that he is innocent of any such lewdness. In his first speech, Eliphaz tapped into a core principle of God's holiness: "As I have seen, those who plow iniquity and sow trouble reap the same." Of course, Eliphaz had misapplied this principle of justice to the case at hand since Job's adversity was not due to his plowing iniquity or sowing trouble. Yet Job recognizes that the principle itself is nonetheless true. Were he guilty of improper sexual desire he would face the Almighty's righteous indictment.

Some might respond, "But we're talking here only of the hypothetical. Job merely speaks of lustful thoughts, not of the actual sin. Just thinking these things is not the same as practicing them." Remember James' observation, though. Lust gives birth to sin. When Eve saw—that is, thoughtfully considered—the appeal of the forbidden fruit, she ate. Jesus reminds us that, "From within, out of the heart of man, come evil thoughts [and] sexual immorality. . . ." The effects may not be as evident, at least at the time, but what we think is as much a part of our character as what we do.

WHO WILL EVER KNOW?

Incentive for Job's resolve to stay clear of lust also comes from his awareness that nothing is hidden from God's sight. Even as he pledges that his eyes will not pore over a woman, Job knows God's eyes discern his deepest thoughts. This insight has already served Job well in his suffering. The fact that "God knows the way that I take" prompts him to anticipate his ultimate vindication. Here as well Job can assert his innocence before all, even *Shaddai* Himself, because his record is clear—and he knows that God knows the truth.

Though his friends accuse him out of their lack of accurate knowledge, Job confesses that God "numbers" all of his steps. He anticipates the words of the psalmist who testifies of the Lord, "You know when I sit down and when I rise up . . . you search out my path and my lying down and are acquainted with all my ways. Even before a word is on my tongue, behold, O LORD, you know it altogether." God's intimate, detailed knowledge scans Job's whole life and turns up no lust, no indelicate, longing gaze toward another woman.

WHAT WE FACE: "I KNOW YOU WANT MY BODY"

The very notion of such a commitment as Job's renouncing lust is ludicrous to most people today. People snickered when President Jimmy Carter once admitted to having lusted in his heart. Keep in mind, though, that Job expresses a view of sexuality reflecting the truth of how God designed the role of sex in our lives. Our culture is the one out of step, having twisted one of His best gifts to humans into an ugly, cheapened sideshow attraction that degrades human personality and shatters human relationships.

Consider how today's world overdoses on lust. Popular media outlets thrive on celebrating sex in any and every form. From *Desperate Housewives* to *Sex in the City* and *Spike TV*, the cable television industry feeds on "giving the public what it wants" of naked bodies, raunchy dialogue, and in-your-face sex talk. Rappers and rockers glorify perversity in blatantly vile lyrics and disgusting visual images. The pop artist Beyoncé Knowles declared with bravado, "I'm feelin' kind of N—A—S—T—Y . . . I know you want my body . . . I see you look me up and down."

It's no surprise in this climate of publicly-indulged and funded lewdness that pornographers have mainstreamed their filth. Even teens casually toss around the jargon of sexual slang the way they discuss *X-Box* and *iPod* downloads. This becomes the very "air" kids breathe through exposure to thousands of *MTV* and *VH-1* depictions of sexual scenes and dialogue. A study by the Henry J. Kaiser Family Foundation concluded that 70% of 15- to 17-year-olds in the United States have viewed pornography online. If young people wade through such a culture of filth, what is the status of our society as a whole when it comes to issues of promiscuous sex? What does it say about our "civilized," decorous, suburban mores when a city in the "Bible Belt" can host the production of a pornographic movie in which some 6,000 men were invited to engage in immorality with one woman?

We have not merely blurred the lines of morality and shoved consideration of right and wrong to the margins; we have blown them apart with a full assault on God's intent for sexuality and left our culture staggering in its wake. The danger facing believers is that we will shake our heads in disgust, wag our finger and say, "naughty, naughty," and go on our way presuming that we have survived this tsunami unscathed by its devastation. We have not. Most assuredly, we are affected. The massive scale of the sexual onslaught dulls our sensitivity to both the beauty of sex and the horror of depravity. Rightly—biblically—understood, physical intimacy and all the wonder it brings are God's holy gift to a husband and a wife. When we defile this gift, we slight God's glory and desecrate His image within us. Thus Job's commitment to purity of thought must take on high priority for all who are serious about a life of integrity.

WHAT WE MUST DO: BUILD THE WALL HIGH

We need a realistic but effective plan of action to honor God and keep lust at bay in our thinking. Work at these seven action steps:

1. COMMIT TO CHRIST ACROSS THE BREADTH OF YOUR ENTIRE LIFE. Purity of thought comes as part of a life-encompassing package. A disciple's walk is a total personality makeover, a transformation in progress in which we give our bodies to God and allow Him to change the way we think. Sexuality is a key segment of our walk, but it takes its place as only one part of the larger picture of a Christian lifestyle. It is not the primary thing in life despite what our culture may suggest. Through the daily practice of spiritual disciplines such as prayer, Bible study and meditation, confession, fellowship, and worship, we submit our lives to God in continuous renewal.

2. WORK TO SHAPE ALL OF YOUR THINKING AROUND BIBLICAL TRUTH. Our goal must be to "take every thought captive to obey Christ." To achieve this goal, we have to take the accompanying step of "punishing every disobedience" when our thoughts cross the line onto unholy turf. One way to work at this goal is to replace those sordid thoughts with wholesome ones. This discipline is tough and takes constant, unyielding attention, but is worth the effort. John Piper, for example, suggests thinking immediately of Christ and His cross when confronted with a sexually arousing image or thought. Train your mind to default to prayer or to Bible meditation when wrong passions intrude. Have some "go to" verses hidden in your heart to re-boot your focus on right thinking.

3. TOTALLY DEFER TO SCRIPTURE IN ALL YOU DO. Not just our thinking, but all that we do must take its shape from the truth of the Bible. Make real in your life what it says about purity, holiness, loyalty, and sex within marriage. Once you have owned these words of wisdom for yourself, hold to them. Don't bring them up for review on the basis of what secular culture dictates.

4. UNDERSTAND GOD'S PURPOSE FOR YOUR BODY WITHIN HIS BODY. We set in motion one of the best safeguards against impure thinking and living when we embrace what the Bible teaches about indwelling. God lives within us through the Holy Spirit as we live within Him as members of His body. His intent is that we glorify Him in our bodies. It only makes sense, then, to "flee" immorality by avoiding whatever would lead us to degrade His body. Our sexual appetites are not evil in and of themselves. God made our bodies with the physical desires that come with them. Like all of His gifts, however, we enjoy their fullest joy only as we submit them to His purposes.

5. PUT HIGH VALUE ON EXERCISING SELF-CONTROL. You will have to summon all the resources at your disposal in Christ to fight this battle constantly. Resolve to live an ordered life under the Spirit's control. Do it today, then tomorrow, then the day after. We dedicate our lives to God not so much in large, "thousand dollar" donations of those huge spiritual decisions, but in the nickels and dimes of each day, in those moments and ordinary thoughts and tasks that make up the substance of our living. Don't allow those moments to slip from the Spirit's control or let yourself off the hook easily by excusing frequent immoral thoughts as "only natural" when we have supernatural assistance to help us order our lives.

6. NEVER FORGET WHERE LUST CAN LEAD. Emulate Joseph who saw lust for where it was headed: toward "sin and great wickedness against God." Each of us knows our weaknesses, so we must stay away at all costs from what gets us into trouble. "Make no provision for the flesh, to gratify its desires," counsels Paul. Build your wall of protection high, whatever that means in your experience: avoiding certain web sites, suggestive language and clothing, certain friends and hangouts, inappropriate touching—you know where you need to steer clear. Choose a believing friend and hold yourself accountable within the Christian community.

Thank God He provides forgiveness and cleansing from sexual impurity. We all fail at times in our struggle with lust, and the Lord provides a way to begin the quest for purity anew. Confess your weakness and count on His compassion through Christ to bring restoration. But we dare not presume on grace with a casual attitude toward what offends God's holiness. To be sure, we glorify God both when we claim forgiveness and when we stay away from sin in the first place. Why not magnify His grace by an intentional commitment to holiness in avoiding wrong and pursuing right? Worse still, what if the chance for forgiveness never comes?

7. CONCENTRATE YOUR THINKING ON HOW BEAUTIFUL PURITY IS. Ridiculed by those who know little of the joy it brings, purity is abandoning ourselves to one pursuit, one course, by taking highest aim at living God's holiness for His glory. A regimen of rugged, beat-down-the-flesh determination will not in and of itself produce purity, however. Relying solely on our own self-control often causes us to fail because our sinful nature is still around to exploit our weakness. Yet while God does exhort us to keep our bodies in check, He also provides us with His lavish, over-the-top grace that works to change us into the likeness of His Son. No wonder Jesus commends the "pure in heart, for they shall see God."

The Honesty Promise:

Job Resolves to Be Truthful before God

Job 31:5–6

If I have walked with falsehood
and my foot has hastened to deceit;
(Let me be weighed in a just balance,
and let God know my integrity!)

In Cormac McCarthy's *No Country for Old Men*, West Texas Sheriff Ed Tom Bell wrestles with fact and fiction in his family history: "The stories gets passed on and the truth gets passed over. As the sayin goes." He continues:

> *Which I reckon some would take as meanin that the truth cant compete. But I dont believe that. I think that when the lies are all told and forgot the truth will be there yet. It dont move about from place to place and it dont change from time to time. You cant corrupt it any more than you can salt salt. You cant corrupt it because that's what it is. It's the thing you're talkin about. I've heard it compared to the rock—maybe in the bible—and I wouldnt disagree with that. But it'll be here even when the rock is gone. (sic)*

Imagine a day in your life totally void of truth. You can't trust your alarm clock, what your wife tells you, the friend you're meeting at Starbucks, the traffic signals, the reports you review at work, the physician who wrote your prescription or the pharmacist who filled it, your teen's word about his evening plans—every word, every expression is suspect. Without truth, life as we know it does not exist.

All of life teaches us that God designed our personalities for truth just as surely as He built our bodies for oxygen. "Falsehood is in itself mean and culpable," remarks Aristotle, "and the truth noble and full of praise." Job, though, knew all about truth. Honesty wrote the first chapter in his story of integrity. Sadly, our culture hasn't read the story—or if it has, we've failed to learn the lesson it teaches.

WHAT JOB SAYS: A CLEAN BILL OF HONESTY

Though some people con their way through life, playing whatever role suits them to get what they want, Job isn't one of them. In verses five and six he denies living a lie. His disclaimer comes in a conditional statement: "If I have walked with falsehood, and my feet have hastened to deceit . . ." Job then appeals for a check-up—a thorough examination from God Himself to give him a clean bill of honesty.

The first phrase of Job's denial uses a metaphor common throughout the Bible. "Walking" often paints a picture of life as a journey, making progress along a path. Our lifestyle is our "walk," biblically speaking. Job declares that he has not "walked with falsehood." Though he has enjoyed many companions in his life, deceit has never been his friend. Honesty came to mind when the people he knew thought of Job.

Yet the word he uses here takes this particular feature of Job's integrity to a higher level. When he denies "falsehood," he means more than just the fact that he didn't tell fibs. The Hebrew word speaks of that which is empty, unreal, and worthless, much like the term translated "vanity" in Ecclesiastes. A "false" thing hides "hollowness under a concealing mask," Franz Delitzsch explains. "You shall not take the name of the LORD your God in vain," insists the third word of the Decalogue. The word "vain" is the same one Job uses—"falsehood." In fact, he has used it earlier, describing the "months of emptiness" which have devastated him, as well as the black hole which swallows the wicked person.

NO "TOP SPIN"

Reinforcing his claim, Job says that he has not run after "deceit." Picture these two scenes he portrays. In the first, Job has not strolled at leisure in the company of falsehood. He now adds, "And I have not chased after a lie." The word "deceit" tightens the net on "falsehood" in the previous line. While the latter is more general, "deceit" comes from a root that speaks of deliberate lying. It shows up in the story of Jacob's misleading Esau, as well as in the Psalms where it describes evil people whose mouths are full of lies. A shifty merchant will use "lying" scales illegally miscalibrated so as to swindle his customer.

In fact, Job borrows this idea of a "balance" or scales as the basis for his plea that God examine his life. Were the Lord to take a close, impartial look at him, Job knows what the findings would show. God is pleased when He looks at Job's heart, and what is there is what Job wants Him to see. He is still a man of integrity. He has not shaded the truth for his own advantage. What a remarkable claim! Who would not expect a man in Job's position, a wealthy businessman with enough power and influence to get whatever he wanted, to cheat or "spin" his way to stay on top? Many CEOs and magnates in our culture are certainly "economical with the truth" and sometimes get caught. Not *this* executive, though. Job commits himself to truth.

WHAT WE FACE: "ALT.ETHICS"

I think it's safe to say that today "honesty is on the ropes."

Ralph Keyes may be right in labeling our day as the "post-truth era." Not that there's anything new about people lying, mind you. Deception has plagued the human family since Eden. The problem today is that many condone and even commend dishonesty. "It's now as acceptable to lie as it is to exceed the speed limit in driving. Nobody thinks twice about it." We've even hedged in our vocabulary. A lie is just "spin," "nuanced truth," "alternative reality," "creative enhancement," "nonfull disclosure," "virtual truth," or a "counterfactual statement."

SURVIVOR TACTICS

This bent to deceive infects our society across the board. Two Jim Carrey movie roles offer cases-in-point regarding our conflicted views on truth-telling. In 1997's *Liar, Liar*, Carrey plays a tortured lawyer condemned to tell nothing but the truth for twenty-four hours. Heaven forbid that anyone should ever really do such a thing! A year later he is salesman Truman Burbank in *The Truman Show*. Though he doesn't know it, his own life is a television show with the whole country looking in every week. His world is fake, a big lie—nothing more than a giant soundstage. From John Lovett, the loveable pathological liar on *Saturday Night Live*, to the cheating, conniving cutthroats on *Survivor*, media entertainment reflects our double-dealing ways. Country singer Patty Loveless slams her lover, "Blame it on your lyin', cheatin', cold dead beatin', two-timin' double-dealin', mean mistreatin', lovin' heart." Who knows how many *iPod* listeners then cheated her, the composers, and the producers of the song out of royalties by their illegal downloads?

Business executives pad their assets by skirting the law through under-the-table profit skimming or insider stock trading. Bernard Ebbers, CEO of MCI WorldCom, a man who led Bible studies and prayers for his employees, now sits in prison convicted of an eleven billion dollar accounting fraud that led to the largest bankruptcy in U. S. history. Yet "middle-class cheating" runs rampant, too, through insurance fraud, employee theft, tax evasion, résumé padding, and more. What's more, anyone who posts on the Internet just assumes a high degree of online misrepresentation. "Online, the whole idea of 'truth' is completely out the window," admits Michel Marriott.

Everyone in our culture shades the truth, or so it seems. Psychologist Robert Feldman estimates that on the average, a person tells three lies for every ten minutes of conversation. The reasons people deceive are many. Some lie to impress people and others to gain sympathy. We embellish the truth in an attempt to get ahead in life or to get ourselves out of trouble.

FAR FROM THE LAND OF THE HOUYHNHNMS

Even though this "Pinocchio syndrome" has always infected human cultures, our "post-truth" era of alt.ethics—"alternative ethics"—is especially troubling because it seems to represent a deeper, systemic mindset of skepticism which questions the baseline concept of absolute truth altogether. In the past, societal consensus at least condemned falsehood as immoral and censured it as a character flaw.

All too often today, however, it's considered okay to distort truth. As Keyes observes, we often have to use disclaimers to emphasize that we're telling the truth: "quite frankly," "let me be candid," "the truth is," "in all honesty," and "to be perfectly honest," just to name a few. Our culture has so given in to relativism that we don't mind contradictions—lies—as long as they serve our entrenched narcissism. David Nyberg claims that honesty is "morally overrated." We should just accept dishonesty as a fact of life and not worry about it.

The world of the Houyhnhnms, those equine creatures in Gulliver's Travels who had no word for "lie" in their rational, honesty-driven society, is indeed a fairy tale. Never more so, however, than in the 21st century misspeak of alt.ethics. Each of us can do better than the lowered expectations of our culture, though.

WHAT WE MUST DO: "DARE TO BE TRUE"

"I've been miserable for two whole years, and I knew I couldn't live with myself if I didn't come clean with you." My former student slumped in the chair beside my desk and admitted he'd lied about a term paper he hadn't actually written by himself. I commended him for the confession, but deep down feared that a single "I did it" would not break a trail of dishonesty he'd left behind.

We are called to live the truth—and that's a vocation we can fulfill. Here are some places to start.

1. STOP EXCUSING THE LIES YOU TELL—EVEN THE "LITTLE WHITE" VARIETY. Though we think "fibs" are harmless, the more we shade the truth in those details that seem of little consequence the more comfortable we become excusing larger deceptions. Be hard on yourself whenever you're not totally honest. Lauren Slater faked epileptic seizures to attract attention, and then confessed, "I lied and a lie is a sin and a sin is never small, because it's a form of separation from God." She's right.

2. ACCEPT THE FACT THAT A LIFESTYLE OF DECEIVING PEOPLE IS A MARK OF NON-CHRISTIAN BEHAVIOR. "Do not lie to one another, seeing that you have put off the old self with its practices," Paul instructs the Christians at Colossae. The truth in Christ sets us free to live honestly, openly, in all our dealings with people. "Lie not; but let thy heart be true to God," writes George Herbert. "Dare to be true. Nothing can need a lie: A fault, which it needs most, grows two thereby."

3. GET A GRIP ON WHAT YOUR LIES WILL DO TO YOU. You may think that evading the truth will get you out of sticky situations; actually, it does the opposite. Lying complicates life. As Augustine puts it, "When regard for the truth has broken down or even slightly weakened, all things will remain doubtful." The habitual liar loses credibility and lowers his own self-esteem. What's more, he becomes skeptical of what others tell him. David Gill contends, "Lies create an internal contradiction that destroys personal integrity and wholeness; you know the truth but say otherwise." People who lie habitually must keep covering up their secrets, piling up falsehoods until eventually the whole illusion collapses and they are found out.

4. IF YOU LIE HABITUALLY, BELIEVE THAT WITH GOD'S HELP, YOU CAN RE-PROGRAM THE WAY YOU THINK AND BECOME AN HONEST PERSON. Nothing in our personality forces us to lie. We really can change our basic attitude and thought pattern by putting value on honesty. Tell yourself that you are a truthful person, and then practice honest behavior each time you have the chance to lie. At some point, however, we must determine to tell the truth *before* we face the choice to lie. Each person has the chance of eliminating deception from his or her life by making the choice to tell and live the truth.

5. COMMIT TO THE NURTURE AND ACCOUNTABILITY OF A TIGHTLY-KNIT COMMUNITY OF BELIEF. Our impersonal, anonymous, "behind closed doors" culture makes it easier to pretend. It's tough to lie consistently to those who are close to us. Accountability, therefore, is just one reason God has designed us for one another within the body of Christ. I need to be transparent inside my intimate, spiritual circle of *koinonia* and learn to speak the truth in love.

6. CONSISTENTLY DEEPEN YOUR WORLDVIEW BASED ON THE ABSOLUTE TRUTH OF GOD. A person committed to the concept of truth in the changeless person of a sovereign God will practice loyalty to a greater degree than a relativist. For the latter, beliefs and ethics are simply products of convention and culture, and so are always contingent. Keyes notes that "the Old English word *trouthe* signified loyalty, fidelity, and reliability," as in the marriage vow, "I pledge thee my troth." You could count on the person who was "true." His word was good. He would do what he said he would.

In *Crime and Punishment*, Fyodor Dostoevsky portrays the honest character of Raskolnikov's mother, Pulcheria Alexandrovna: ". . . [T]here was always a certain point in her honesty, in her rules of conduct and in her profound convictions beyond which no circumstance in the world could drive her." So it was with Job, who fits well Herbert's description:

> For above all things he abhors deceit;
> His words and works and fashion too
> All of a piece, and all are clear and straight.

Truth is the soul of integrity.

CHAPTER 4

The Contentment Promise:

Job Resolves to Be Satisfied with What He Has

Job 31:7–8, 24–25

If my step has turned aside from the way
and my heart has gone after my eyes,
and if any spot has stuck to my hands,
then let me sow, and another eat,
and let what grows for me be rooted out.

If I have made gold my trust
or called fine gold my confidence
if I have rejoiced because my wealth was abundant
or because my hand had found much,

Steve and Michelle Kirsch enjoyed the life most people envy. The three companies they owned in Silicon Valley afforded them a custom-designed house, fine works of art, and other upper-crust perks. The next step for them? They sold all three businesses for a total of over four billion dollars, started a foundation, and then began giving multiple millions to charity. "You know," Michelle conceded, "you only need so much really to live comfortably."

The Kirsches defy the odds when it comes to how the majority of us in this lottery-crazed, debt-funded age look at wealth. Whether it's shopping at Saks on Fifth Avenue or at Walmart on the bypass, we love to get stuff—after all, we're "living in a material world," Madonna once reminded us. Jerry Maguire's line has become our mantra: "Show me the money!" Reinhold Niebuhr contends that ". . . (W)e are the first culture which is in danger of being subordinated to its economy. We have to live as luxuriously as possible in order to keep our productive enterprise from falling."

In the classic 1948 film *The Treasure of the Sierra Madre*, Howard, the gruff old prospector played by Walter Huston, ominously warns Humphrey Bogart as they set out on their expedition, "I know what gold does to men's souls." So did Job. In verses 7-8 and 24-25 he renounces a love for money in some of the strongest possible language.

WHAT JOB SAYS: CLEAN HANDS, CLEAN HEART

Although Job once held enormous wealth as the richest man in the region, his wealth never held him. Money-making did not drive Job, as two segments of his oath reveal. The first, in verses 7 and 8, follows his denial of living a lie. Its placement here is strategic since greediness itself is a pretentious way to live, looking as it does for reality in "stuff" which is never stable, never reliable. Here Job offers his first full statement of the oath formula: the condition ("if") followed by the consequences ("then"). He vows that should his desire entice him to grab for what he should not have, then as punishment a similar fate should come his way.

Verse seven unfolds in a bookend "A-B-A" pattern. His wayward "step" and dirty "hands" suggest greedy deeds, while the central line these phrases surround—"my heart has gone after my eyes"—points to a greedy motive. Job now asserts once more with identical language what he has affirmed earlier: "My foot has held fast to his steps; I have kept his way and have not turned aside." As in verse four, the image of walking along a straight path conveys the idea of living the proper way before God—the "road par excellence," Robert Gordis calls it. The corresponding line speaks of a "spot" or blemish sticking to Job's hands. Earlier in the book, stained or blackened hands refer to sinful actions while clean hands reflect righteous deeds.

Had Job committed them, such shameful acts would reflect his guilty conscience. His "heart"—his desire—would have "gone after his eyes." This brief phrase captures precisely Eve's experience when she "saw" that the forbidden fruit was a "delight . . . to be desired." Covetous character would have ruined Job long before now. As punishment he would have seen others plunder the produce he had cultivated and should be enjoying himself. "The uprooting of his crops just before harvest would demoralize him, for his long, hard labor done in anticipation of a good harvest would have been in vain," explains John E. Hartley.

GOD, GOODS, AND GOLD

The second segment of Job's denial that a desire for wealth controlled his life comes in verses 24 and 25. While verses seven and eight convey this message in general terms of Job's lifestyle, these lines open a section of the chapter primarily concerned with worship, his ultimate loyalty. The mention of God's "majesty" in verse 23 broaches the subject. Job now uses language often associated with devotion to God. Note the nouns "trust" and "confidence," with the possessive pronoun ("my") attached, followed by the verb "rejoice": "my trust . . . my confidence . . . I have rejoiced." These are usually words we might use as we express our personal devotion to God—worship words! Much to our surprise, though, Job uses them not of God, but of gold!

It would be easy to boast had "my hand found much," Job admits. The Hebrew text here stresses the word "much" in the line's structure: ". . . or because *much* my hand found." Job's mention of his hand suggests his own power to get rich—a claim which would exude pride. Despite the impressive fortune he had amassed and the influence that came with it, Job had never succumbed to the spell so often cast by money.

He again phrases his response in terms of the conditional oath: "If I have made gold my trust, or called fine gold my confidence, if I have rejoiced because my wealth was abundant . . . ," with the consequences following in verse 28. The word translated "wealth" suggests all kinds of power, whether that of money, strength, or influence—"clout," as we might say. Riches and all the control they bring do not control Job. Wealth is not his god. No matter how "much" he had acquired, his "fear of God is (his) confidence," as Eliphaz had suggested earlier. Job exemplifies the blessed man portrayed by David who makes the LORD his trust.

WHAT WE FACE: "MUST BE THE MONEY"

Anyone with a finger to the pulse of our culture knows that money calls all the shots. David Wells labels it "unbridled consumer desire." Mass media and marketers feed our habit to get, then to get more. Though we'd dare not admit it, deep in the darkness of our depravity Michael Douglas' lines from the movie *Wall Street* resonate within us: "Greed . . . is good. Greed is right. Greed works." According to one study, students in Duke University's School of Business desired more than anything to be "money-making machine(s)." We've bought into the promos that tell us we need money's power to buy that 3,500 square-foot home in the upscale neighborhood, drive the Lexus—or the Mercedes, or both—and send our kids to ivy-league universities. In 1982 there were 23 billionaires in the United States; just 14 years later their number had exploded to 132.

Greed's snare entangles not just those who think they have it all, however. In fact, those who have the least and buy into the "get rich quick" infomercials may have the most to fear. Consider the following "advice" from Harv Eker, best-selling author of *Secrets of the Millionaire Mind*:

"You can be a victim *or* you can be rich, but you can't be both."

"Are you willing to work sixteen hours a day . . . seven days a week and give up most of your weekends . . . sacrifice your family, your friends, and give up your recreations and hobbies? Rich people are."

"Rich people hang around winners. Poor people hang around losers."

" . . . (P)eople have bought into the adage, 'It's better to give than to receive.' Let me put this as elegantly as possible: 'What a *crock*!' That statement is total hogwash . . . The whole idea is ludicrous. . . ."

Before his priorities changed, professional athlete "Prime Time Neon" Deion Sanders traveled this road and expressed it in a rap song he wrote entitled "*Must Be the Money!*"

Must be the money that's turning them on;
Must be the money. You know what can go wrong?
Must be the money. That keeps me lookin' cold.
Must be the money. That's got me rollin' on the stroll . . .
I'm livin' large, and you know I can't deny . . .
Must be the money!

NO TASTE IN THE SECOND HELPING

Since our culture basks in "the good life" where per capita income adjusted for inflation has more than doubled over the past forty-five years, you'd think that Americans must be the happiest people anywhere at any time. Think again. Like Santiago in *The Old Man and the Sea*, we've landed the catch of our lives only to find nothing but bare bones when we get it to shore. To paraphrase Oliver Goldsmith, we live in a time when wealth accumulates yet men decay. Regardless of gender or age, individuals consumed with financial success register higher levels of depression and anxiety, studies show.

An obsession with wealth is like a drug addiction but never reaches the "high" it craves. We want more, but when we get it, we're not satisfied. The second helping never tastes as good as the first. When making money becomes the center of our lives, everything we do collapses onto ourselves and we neglect the relationships that connect us to reality. Certainly we want to do well for ourselves and for our family. God designed us to live off the bounty He provides through our work; yet when the "sacred thirst for gold" dominates us to the extent that the only way we think we can quench it is to pull out the plastic, we have relocated self from what satisfies over the long haul to what evaporates as quickly as it comes. Money cannot buy meaning. It means nothing except what we allow it to mean.

THE GOSPEL OF AFFLUENCE

Tragically, the love of money infects the church as well. I recall staying as the guest of a prominent church leader's family in their luxurious home, complete with a two-story waterfall cascading through the foyer. Soon I detected, however, a crippling level of stress casting a shadow over these good people and their relationships with one another. I later learned that pending litigation had tied up their fortune in court and their lifestyle was in jeopardy. It's the truth—Christians mirror our culture when it comes to a consumer-driven mentality, and it shows in our priorities. Based on studies of giving patterns in conservative churches between 1968 and 2001, Ron Sider concludes, "As we got richer and richer, evangelicals chose to spend more and more on themselves and give a smaller and smaller percentage to the church. Today, on average, evangelicals in the United States give about two-fifths of a tithe." Francis Schaeffer was speaking to us when he charged that most of what we spend our lives trying to get will end up on the city dump.

WHAT WE MUST DO: BREAK FREE OF MONEY'S POWER

Dealing with money is a routine but necessary part of life. We can manage it effectively if we apply biblical principles of stewardship.

1. MAKE A CONSCIOUS, CONTINUAL COMMITMENT TO PUT CHRIST FIRST. Surrender your will to the truth that God owns you, and then have the courage to refuse to let popular culture dictate your values. Luther had a point when he claimed that two conversions were necessary: one of our hearts, the other of our pocketbooks. "To love money, to be attached to it, is to hate God," Jacques Ellul charges. God and mammon cannot share the throne. Don't forget Jesus' caution that the desire to become rich carries with it a deadly danger: ". . . only with difficulty will a rich person enter the kingdom of heaven." First century Macedonian Christians modeled this lesson for us. They were able to give their money for God's work because they had first given themselves to Him.

2. REPROGRAM YOUR MINDSET TO THINK CORRECTLY ABOUT MONEY. Although money and material possessions have no value in and of themselves, our attitude toward them, to a great degree, steers the direction of the spiritual disciplines in our lives. How many potential kingdom servants have said "no" to a mission post, a classroom, or a pulpit because the salary couldn't support the lifestyle they envisioned for themselves? Stewardship falls under the umbrella of discipleship. The book of Ecclesiastes, of all places, is an excellent primer for studying a balanced view of wealth. Qoheleth continually reminds us that though God gives good gifts to His people, we must not live for those gifts but for the One who gives them. Yancey's admission speaks to all of us: "I needed to see money for what it is, a loan that God has entrusted to me for the purpose of investing in the kingdom of heaven, the only kingdom that pays eternal dividends."

3. BEGIN BY DENYING YOURSELF SOMETHING YOU WANT—SOMETHING YOU WANT BADLY. In our indulgent age funded by easy credit, we conveniently forget Jesus' call to deny self, to forsake all that we have if necessary to follow Him. Seal that commitment by refusing to buy that "toy" you so desperately want, and let your refusal serve as a token of Christ's lordship over your possessions. We must resist society's "belief that consuming is essential to the nurture of the self." Work hard to live within your means. Use wisdom and avoid getting over your head in debt. Herbert's words are true: "Who cannot live on twenty pound a year, Cannot on forty."

4. GIVE—GIVE EASILY AND CONSTANTLY. Harv Eker is dead wrong about what Jesus says. Greater blessing does come to those whose hearts are open to share with others what God has given them. A greedy heart is a selfish heart. One reason why a sense of community is vital to the Christian is that it extrudes us out of self by reminding us of the expansive scope of God's redemptive mission. In the economy of the church, it's not about parceling out mine for me and yours for you. It's about *koinonia*, what is ours in the common stewardship God lavishes upon us. Giving is thus "the penetration of grace into the world of competition and selling." We must do our best at our work to honor God, to support our families, and to have the means to give to those who are in need. Wealth in and of itself is not a bad thing. The problem comes when "our heart becomes proud in (its) wealth" and we "close our hearts" to the people we could help.

5. CONTENTMENT NEED NOT BE AN IMPOSSIBLE DREAM. LET IT BRING A STABLE SERENITY TO YOUR LIFE. Paul reminds us that contentment is a learning process. We grow into it as we come to view wealth in terms other than money. Make a list of what makes you "rich," leaving out any reference to the things you have bought. My list would include grandchildren; restored health; a soul mate in life; purpose in my work; breathing in Blue Ridge mountain air on a cool, crisp spring morning—on and on I could go, but count your own blessings and then tell God thank you for these treasures. Shakespeare's Portia was right: "He is well paid that is well satisfied."

The first generation Christians learned this lesson well. While they "endured a hard struggle with sufferings, sometimes being publicly exposed to reproach and affliction," the writer of Hebrews commends them saying, "you had compassion on those in prison, and you joyfully accepted the plundering of your property, since you knew that you yourselves had a better possession and an abiding one."

The Loyalty Promise:

Job Resolves to Be Faithful to His Wife

Job 31:9–12

If my heart has been enticed toward a woman,
and I have lain in wait at my neighbor's door,
then let my wife grind for another,
and let others bow down on her.
or that would be a heinous crime;
that would be an iniquity to be punished by the judges;
or that would be a fire that consumes as far as Abaddon,
and it would burn to the root all my increase.

A scene from the TV sitcom *Seinfeld* finds the single George Costanza in bed with a married woman, Robin, whom he's only recently met. When the reality of what has just occurred hits him, George begins the conversation:

George: Oh my God. I must be crazy. What have I done?

Robin: Oh no, what's wrong?

George: What's wrong? I'll tell you what's wrong. I just committed adultery!

Robin: You didn't commit adultery, I did.

George: Oh yeah.

Robin: If I didn't do it with you, I would have done it with someone else.

A large segment of society takes just such a matter-of-fact approach toward infidelity among married people. What was once unthinkable and whispered as rumor over tea in gilded parlors now has almost zero shock value. That's not to say, however, that adultery is in vogue for most people. Statistics show that from 21 to 33% of husbands and 11 to 25% of wives are unfaithful to their spouses. Every major civilized society in history has recognized the practice as aberrant, unacceptable behavior. Our culture is not yet willing to say that cheating on a partner is okay. Clearly, though, our 21st century attitudes have softened toward the subject. Though adultery is still technically illegal in twenty-six states, few magistrates enforce these codes today.

So what's the big deal? Adultery is not a page-one concern anymore—until it happens to you or to someone you love. Then its savagery becomes all too evident. What caught our curiosity on *Jerry Springer* or in a checkout line tabloid is not as coy or intriguing as it once was. We then see it for the odious plunderer it is—how it disfigures marriage, violates trust, and jettisons self-esteem in its wake.

Did such a notion of "greener pastures" ever appeal to Mr. or Mrs. Job? It often does to people who are in the midst of devastating loss, as they were. Not only had his fortune, his health, and his community standing deserted Job, but his family was also decimated. All ten children were lying in their graves. Think of the magnitude of that blow. His intimate family circle was no more. All of his experiences with his seven boys and the special delight he took in that trio of daughters—nothing remained except memories.

And now his sweetheart, his bride, tells him to "curse God and die." She had suffered as he had, but it hit her harder. She hadn't handled it well. Her children, her stricken husband, her security—no doubt her dreams were dashed to pieces. What will she do? Will she leave him for someone less disaster-prone? When—if—he recovers, will he stay with her after what she said? No wonder Job broaches the subject of staying in his marriage.

WHAT JOB SAYS: "THY NEIGHBOR'S WIFE"

Though he is on the pyre of suffering, Job has enough regard for his wife and their marriage to assert his commitment to fidelity. Verses 9-12 present his claim in the full "if . . . then" formula of the oath. His explanation of the supposed offense is somewhat cryptic. In these two parallel "what if" statements, he never comes right out to speak of "adultery" per se. Instead he alludes to the seductive trap laid by the would-be adulteress and the ensuing steps her partner might take to make the affair happen. She begins to weave her web with an appeal to his desire, his "heart," a theme we noted in verse one. Like the seductive temptress in Proverbs, no doubt she entices him with her "smooth words." The verb "entice" occurs in other contexts where sexual allurement is involved.

Should he fall for her charms, this wayward husband would look for an opportunity to be with her and to satisfy his stirred desire. The second line in verse nine describes just such an attempt. Apparently, as Job pictures the scene, the "woman" is a neighbor's wife. In ancient cities and villages, large families lived in dwellings which physically adjoined each other; making a rendezvous such as the one Job envisions a difficult feat to carry out. Ironically, in Proverbs 7, the woman "lies in wait" to meet her lover. Here, he spies out the situation for his chance to be with her, probably when her husband and the rest of her family leave. Job's point, of course, is that no such scenario has ever occurred in his life. He denies having done such a despicable deed, perhaps reflecting again on the truth he introduced earlier: "The eye of the adulterer also waits for the twilight, saying, 'No eye will see me'; and he veils his face." Some husbands may betray their wives' trust, but Job avows that he is not one of them.

FLAMING INFIDELITY

Had Job cheated on his wife, deep and terrible consequences would have engulfed both of them. The fact that she faced such indignant shame because of his crime offends our 21st century notions of fair play. Why should she suffer when he's such a cad? We need to look through the lens of Job's culture around 2000 B. C., however, to make sense of verse 11. Mrs. Job's resulting abuse at the hands of another man actually constituted judgment against both her *and* her husband since ancient Near Eastern peoples thought of marriage partners as a single entity. Husband and wife were one; they not only lived together, the destiny and identity of each one were also bound up in the other. This notion of corporate responsibility shows up several times in the Old Testament. Job himself would suffer intense disgrace should his wife go through such despair.

In another sense, what happens in verse ten may not be all that strange to us when we consider that adultery devastates both partners today, even so-called "innocent" parties. Everyone in the family and in a wider circle of friends suffers when a spouse proves unfaithful to a mate.

Mrs. Job's fate due to her husband's sin would find her doing the menial work of a slave for another man, "grinding" grain at his mill to make bread. The picture of other men "bowing down" or crouching over her may refer to sexual degradation she endures at their hands—sort of a retaliatory, "eye-for-an-eye" judgment sentence upon his infidelity. Since he has violated another man's wife, now his own wife suffers in kind. This horrific picture actually offers a strong defense of Job's innocence since it is unthinkable that any decent man, let alone a man of proven integrity, would knowingly bring such a curse upon his wife.

Verse 11 rightly labels adultery "a heinous crime." The Hebrew word behind this translation speaks of repugnant sexual sins such as incest and prostitution. Such behavior is "iniquity," perversion of the worst sort. It stands not only as an offense in God's sight but also constitutes a violation of any sensible standard of human decency. "The judges," civil magistrates charged with enforcing civil codes of conduct, rightly find that such treachery in the most vital and intimate of all mortal relationships shreds the fabric of all that is right.

From this devastation emerges a fire that ravages the wayward husband, leaving a scorched trail smoldering all the way to the grave (verse 12). "Abaddon" (literally "destruction") is a synonym for *sheol*, the place and experience of the dead. The flames consume him as well as his profit, destroying every good thing he has in this life and threatening his welfare in the next. Job sees adultery as that fire a man "carries next to his chest," those "hot coals" that most surely will scorch his feet and lead him to the "chambers of death."

WHAT WE FACE: THE BONDS OF "SEXUAL FREEDOM"

As reflected in the above-mentioned *Seinfeld* scene, pop entertainment culture teases us with sometimes sensational, sometimes "hush-hush" escapades suggesting that extra-marital pursuits are the norm for "hip" people. The subject has long fascinated us, whether in history, music, or literature. We read of Benjamin Franklin's indiscretions and Thomas Jefferson's infidelity with Sally Hemmings. Wagner's *Tristan and Isolde* portray the theme in opera. *Madame Bovary*, *Anna Karenina*, and *The Scarlet Letter* depict the soulful stories of affairs with all their bitter complexities.

Recent years have offered *Fatal Attraction*, *American Beauty*, and *The English Patient* in big-screen versions of marital philandering. The Internet brings "meet to cheat" and "consenting adulterers" websites into our dens and offices. To soften the effect, we try to avoid the guilt-ridden harshness of the very word "adultery." It comes across as too puritanical, too stark for our postmodern sensibilities. Instead we toss around euphemisms, such as "sleeping around" (with little to do with sleep!), fooling around, affairs, flings, and dalliances. Athletes, princes, celebrities, even presidents partake. It all sounds so innocent, so blasé to our jaded ears.

Yet our culture is actually conflicted over the issue. Awareness of adultery's impact can be beneficial—that is, if our awareness sees the true nature of infidelity and in this caveat lies the problem.

As with most sin, Alexander Pope reminds us, "seen too oft, and familiar with her face, we first endure, then pity, then embrace." Society celebrates "sexual freedom," the right to find self-fulfillment for one's libido whenever and with whomever we choose. When people try to do that, however, the consequences often overwhelm them.

CLEANING UP THE MESS

None of us escape adultery's effects. Our callous, "so what?" attitude causes us to disengage, in varying degrees, from our partner and from our commitment to make our marriage the best it can be. We drift into indifference and negligence toward those who matter the most to us *even though we've never had an affair*. It's awfully tough, too, to keep our hearts stoked with a fire for God when sin's deceitfulness hardens us.

Many partners who would never have physical intercourse outside their wedding vows fall into the trap of emotional adultery. A close friend becomes an intimate to a dangerous degree while our partner suffers inattention and senses betrayal as an icy pallor descends upon the relationship. Suspicion becomes withdrawal and even depression. Two strangers who once were lovers at the deepest levels reside together while they live apart. Christians need a stout slap in the face to rouse us from our denial. Adultery can visit stable, apparently idyllic homes. In fact, it drops in all the time because we leave the front door wide open. The affair may eventually end, but it leaves great loss—of trust, self-esteem, security, reputation, honor, and the sacred joy that attends a godly marriage.

If you doubt the still-present stigma of adultery, look into the moistened eyes of its victim. Hear her lament and follow the tears. Feel the anguished guilt and hurt of his broken spirit. Friends have told me it's the same feeling you have when someone you love dies, only worse. At least most deaths are not stained with betrayal.

WHAT WE MUST DO: WEAVING THE FABRIC OF LOYALTY

We're kidding ourselves if we assume that faithfulness in our lives and in our marriages is just a "given." Fidelity starts with keeping a close watch over how we think about God and what we promise Him. It then works itself into a daily quest to keep those promises. Let these principles help you.

1. CULTIVATE THE PRIMAL LOYALTY: WALK WITH GOD. The stories of professing Christians who have betrayed their spouses almost always have a common theme. Before they broke their vows to their mate, they broke their vows to God. Those "little foxes" really do "spoil the vines." Inattention to the exercises God gives us for our spiritual fitness starts the slide. We miss our meetings with Him in prayer. We "skip school" when it comes to His instruction in the Word. We shy away from our community of support and accountability—Christ's body, the church. If you read key Bible passages dealing with sexual impurity, you'll notice embedded in their context is often a challenge to us that we mature through communion with God, with His Word, and with His people in a lifestyle of worship.

2. LET SCRIPTURE CALL THE SHOTS IN EVERYTHING THAT PERTAINS TO YOU AND YOUR FAMILY. I once heard it said of a devoted servant-teacher of the Lord's people that "his mind was formed by the word of God." May that description fit you and me! Since the Bible comes from God and reveals His supreme wisdom, its authority trumps our whimsical feelings and our culture's fickle trends. When He warns that adultery will "burn" you, believe it. If you find yourself excusing fantasies you're having about a co-worker, think again about where that road leads. Look ahead and see your shame, your family's hurt and embarrassment, the damage to your career, and your betrayal of God Himself.

3. UNDERSTAND WHAT LOVE REALLY IS AND LIVE IN THAT LOVE. Infidelity is rooted in selfishness. True love, though—biblical love—commits itself to the interest of others and gives whatever is required for the good of the one we love. Love is not about sleek, buff bodies and the shallow, sensate allure of one-night stands. In love's world, the husband does the housework for his wife then holds her after those draining chemotherapy treatments. In love's world she still wouldn't have any other man on the planet though the years have loosened his belt and his hair, and she still tells him so. Whatever happens—his job falls through, their daughter dies, she develops Alzheimer's—love "bears all things" and "endures all things." It never fails.

4. CULTIVATE LOYALTY IN ALL AREAS OF YOUR LIFE. Keeping one promise, however small, has a way of spilling over into other commitments. Pretty soon you realize you're becoming a loyal person, and you feel good about yourself and what others see in you. From little promises kept grows a pattern of fidelity and a lifestyle of trust. Follow through today in those roles where people are counting on you. Show up today, as you promised.

5. RECOGNIZE THE ROLE OF PLEASURE IN MARRIAGE FOR WHAT IT REALLY IS. What delicious irony we find tucked away in the fabric of loyalty! The routines of marriage we often consider so boring as to spark notions of "real" pleasure we think we'll find with someone else actually house the real pleasure themselves. As Lauren Winner observes, we find "excitement . . . in the stable, daily—and yes, occasionally dull— rhythms of marriage." Faithfulness between a wife and her husband cast all of those routines—paying the bills, changing the diapers, fixing the house, making love, and the rest—in the best light of all: blessings from the hand of a faithful God who satisfies us with what is good. We never know true intimacy apart from the security commitment provides.

6. RESOLVE CONFLICTS WITH YOUR SPOUSE BEFORE THEY DOMINATE YOUR RELATIONSHIP. The stressors of life make skirmishes in a marriage inevitable. Yet when those irritants persist without resolution, they may nudge a partner closer and closer to infidelity. Whether it's over a job, the in-laws, money, the kids, pet peeves, or just plain stubbornness, one of you must throw in the towel and climb out of the ring before this sparring turns into a knockout and the injuries find soothing from someone else. Stop arguing and solve the problem while you can.

7. SET HIGH DEFENSES AGAINST CHEATING. Make it your goal to be for your partner everything he or she needs. Don't take her for granted. Esteem her highly. Fuss over her and treat her royally. Avoid comparing him with the guy down the street who constantly works on his house and grooms his lawn to perfection. Guard against "innocent" flirting someone may take the wrong way and make more of than you intended. Know what "traps" ensnare you; watch out for them, and steer clear. Convince yourself that no one, not even you, is exempt from lapses in loyalty.

8. WHEN/IF INFIDELITY HAS OCCURRED, THE THREE HEALING STEPS ARE REPENTANCE, RECONCILIATION, AND FORGIVENESS. One careless decision need not ruin a life or destroy a marriage as long as a careful decision follows: the choice of repentance. To repent is not just to feel sorry—sorry for what you did or, especially, sorry that you got caught. Genuine repentance reprograms our way of thinking and breaks a patterned disposition of unfaithfulness. We learn to detest cheating; fidelity becomes a comfortable fit for us. God's reconciling love paves the way for a new beginning with those we have violated. Jesus forgave the woman caught in adultery, and He can furnish us with grace to forgive each other.

CHAPTER 6

The Equity Promise:

Job Resolves to Be Fair to Others

Job 31:13–15

If I have rejected the cause of
my manservant or my maidservant,
when they brought a complaint against me,
what then shall I do when God rises up?
When he makes inquiry, what shall I answer him?
Did not he who made me in the womb make him?
And did not one fashion us in the womb?

A Cajun mob hankers to lynch Mathu. The black man stands accused of murdering Beau Bouton, a well-to-do farmer in the Louisiana bayou. In defense of their friend, eighteen old black men show up, each carrying a shotgun and each claiming that he killed Bouton. Questions of justice and equality and deep-rooted prejudices tangle the back-and-forth charges leveled in Ernest J. Gaines' *A Gathering of Old Men*. Gil Bouton, the dead man's brother, offers a claim of reason:

"Those days are gone, Papa," Gil said, "Those days when you just take the law in your own hands—those days are gone. These are the '70s, soon to be the '80s. Not the '20s, the '30s, or the '40s. People died—people we knew—died to change those things. Those days are gone forever, I hope."

If only this were a world of perfect justice. If people would just do right by each other—it sounds so simple, or at least it seems that way when you read mass-market legal thrillers or watch big-screen crime dramas. Richard Kimble, *The Fugitive*, protests, "I didn't kill my wife!" He didn't, and it all works out in the end, much to the dismay of the one-armed man who did kill her. We long for a fair deal and "crave the explicit, dogmatic, and final rendering of justice, which is always fiction's task, never life's," says Terry White.

The truth is that only a biblical worldview furnishes the adequate materials for building a system of justice. Job's fair treatment of his servants supports that claim. So, too, does the Bible's larger teaching on justice. In fact, later history reveals that true Christian practice always brings with it a surge in equal rights. The demise of slavery, for example, in the ancient world as well as the modern resulted primarily from "the theological conclusion that slavery is sinful" contributed by biblical religion. Christianity's "belief in moral equality . . . has informed Western political and legal practices guaranteeing equality before the law and many other forms of equal rights." Still each of us wrestles with how to be fair to the people we meet today on our corner of the planet.

WHAT JOB SAYS: "JUSTICE FOR ALL"

In Job's culture some four thousand years ago wealthy landowners used slaves in their workforce. Their economy depended on this conscripted labor pool, and Job was no exception. "Very many servants" worked for him, we're told. It comes as no surprise that slaves often endured much abuse at the hands of their masters since many ancient Near Eastern law codes classed servants as mere property. Yet here Job broke ranks with the norm of his day. In verses 13-15 he boldly asserts that he has treated his servants with equity and justice. Two reasons have prompted Job's fair dealings with them. First, he knows that he himself must answer to God as the Lord's own servant; and second, he understands that no essential difference exists between himself and his laborers. God has created all people in His divine image.

PLAINTIFFS VS. JOB

Although the text tells us of no specific incidents, Job asserts in verse 13 that he has listened to the complaints of his servants and has responded fairly to them. Legal concepts recur in these verses. The word translated "cause" shows up throughout the Old Testament to denote a legal action or case. Its root meaning has to do with justice—a sense of right and fair play issuing from the character of God Himself. Bildad, Elihu, and Job testify to God's equity in the book. In this verse the idea apparently involves a legal case in which Job's servants have claimed that he has wronged them. As we might say, they "filed suit" against him.

The idea of a lawsuit fits the context well given the repeated use of this word "complaint" in the book. Job has repeatedly sought a "hearing" with God, a face-to-face courtroom showdown, as it were, in which he would try to defend himself in light of the charges God apparently had leveled against him. He now uses this concept in his oath of innocence to illustrate his sense of fairness toward everyone, including those typically considered beneath him in the social strata. Therefore he did not simply shrug off these claims as frivolous and reject them because his slaves were the ones making the accusations. On the contrary, Job had even taken seriously the concerns of his *female* slaves whose legal standing in most cultures would have been nil compared to their male counterparts, who were, after all, only bondsmen themselves.

ONE JUDGE, ONE CREATOR

Verses 14 and 15 present two reasons for Job's evenhanded treatment of his servants. He realizes, first of all, that God will evaluate his own life and require an answer for all of his actions, including his response to these charges. The repetition of "what" catches our eye in verse 14: *What* will I do when God "rises up" to judge me? *What* will I say in response to His close inspection of my actions? Had he mistreated his servants, Job would have faced a just God who would have passed sentence on this inequity.

We find the second cause in verse 15—a remarkable verse Hartley says is "ahead of (its) time" for an ethic "unmatched in the ancient world" regarding human nature. Although not evident in most English translations, this verse displays a concentric A-B-B'-A' layout in the original language. Two different rhyming Hebrew terms for "womb" surround parallel statements describing God's prenatal artistry in creating human beings: "he who made me . . . made him" and "did not one fashion us." Job has already marveled at God's delicate design of the infant in the womb. Now he extends the inference of divine oversight in the process of gestation to its logical social ethic. Every human reflects the image of the Creator and is a person of infinite worth no matter who he or she is.

WHAT WE FACE: OBSTRUCTION OF JUSTICE

McCoy isn't Mason. Sam Waterston's character on the television series *Law and Order* just didn't seem to get those (admittedly cheesy) last-minute courtroom confessions like Perry Mason could. Sometimes the guilty even go free in today's ambiguous legal dramas; 21st century justice seems so muddled, so conflicted. "Discrimination!" "It's not fair!" Cries of injustice fly at press conferences and on picket lines just as they do on playgrounds when we think that someone has dealt us a bum hand. All of us, kids included, come equipped with a hair-triggered fairness detector ready to go off immediately when we sense mistreatment. Even though our instincts are honed for equity, our application of this principle in real life is often skewed due to that not-so-little problem we have called depravity.

CREATED EQUAL

The irony is that the only people in the world who can freely claim injustices are those who live in a society where laws provide a large helping of justice. From Plato and Aristotle to Thomas Aquinas to the United States Declaration of Independence, Western societies forged by democratic ideals have tapped into a universal principle of justice "beyond human will," a transcendent "self-evident" absolute of fairness which weighs human action. Because God designed us in His image, every person deserves respectful, even-handed treatment from every other person.

Skin color, nationality, gender, economic status, or religion—these variables should not deprive any person of an opportunity for housing, an education, a career, or fulfilling his or her ambitions for the best life. Likewise justice must provide the pre-born, the mentally challenged, and the physically disabled with the right to live and to enjoy a life with the fullest meaning that a fair allocation of resources can give. The degree of success will vary according to individuals, of course. Treating people fairly does not necessarily mean treating them equally. Some will achieve higher goals, and rightly so because skill, aptitude, ambition, and perseverance vary from one person to another even though all people share common human dignity and worth.

SHOVING "SELFISH GENES"

Although Western culture traditionally has embraced this higher notion of justice as an objective reality, dissenting opinions not only threaten its pride of place but challenge its very existence as well. One voice raised in opposition comes from the relatively new field of "evolutionary psychology." Edward O. Wilson, Peter Singer, Robert Wright, and others have applied Darwin's theory of natural selection to the realm of brain development and cognition. They conclude that the realm of human ideals—compassion, altruism, esthetics, and most relevant here, justice—stem from our survival instincts and signal the presence of a "selfish gene." Wright's statements represent this view: "The intuitively obvious idea of just deserts, the very core of the human system of justice, is . . . a by-product of evolution, a simple genetic stratagem."

Our notion of fairness, they claim, is simply our genetic coping mechanism working to further self-interest. Job's consideration of his servants, then, was nothing more than a subconscious stratagem to earn him more "brownie points" toward long term viability. Wright concludes,

> The eternal sense that retribution embodies some higher ethical truth . . . is harder to credit once (it) is seen to be a self-serving message from our genes, not a beneficent message from the heavens. Its origin is no more heavenly than that of hunger, hatred, lust, or any other things that exist by virtue of their past success in shoving genes through generations.

THE GENES OUT OF THE BOTTLE

Many of Singer's horrific proposals, selective infanticide, for example, represent "just" measures: "The fact that a human being is a human being . . . is not relevant to the wrongness of killing it. . . ." The interests of society or the dominant force in a population represent evolution's way of determining justice. The problem is that this perspective paves the way for racism, genetic manipulation, economic oppression, religious persecution, genocide, and all sorts of mass abuse flying under the flag of "justice" as defined by naturalism.

As Charles Colson notes, when legal authority rests on nothing other than the prevalent trends of society, neither justice nor injustice is relevant any longer. "Either we are created, and the law is the law because its reference point is the Creator, or this is a godless universe, and law is merely what humans from time to time decide it is—because there is nothing else for it to be." When society jettisons an absolute, final standard of justice, ". . . law is based on nothing more than the perceived needs of the moment."

Recent judicial activism in the United States has reflected this philosophy. Social custom, not a fixed code of law—the

Constitution in our case—all too often determines what today's rules are. Nancy Pearcey quotes Oliver Wendell Holmes, Jr., a legal pragmatist: "The justification for any given law, Holmes wrote, is 'not that it represents an eternal principle,' such as Justice, but 'that it helps bring out a social end which we desire.'" Holmes' philosophy pervades much of our present legal system and illustrates society's quandary over the issue of justice. We know injustice when we see it, but postmodern culture tells us it's all relative: what you take as a wrong is someone else's right and both of you are really victims.

WHAT WE MUST DO: DON'T FUDGE ON THE WARRANTY

Too often when we think of "justice" we only consider it in the larger political and legal arenas. While God's people do need to involve themselves on that scale, treating people fairly touches our lives every day in ordinary ways.

1. LIVE DAY-BY-DAY, ACT-BY-ACT, WITH THE KNOWLEDGE THAT WE REAP WHAT WE SOW. Although his friends were wrong about the reason Job was suffering, he knew well that God holds us accountable for our deeds since He is a just God. He calls our hand when we think too much of ourselves and demean others. The flip side of this principle should spur us on to give our best in all that we do. We know the Lord rewards faithfulness. "Do you see the great importance God places on . . . standing up for those who have been treated unjustly?" asks Chrysostom. "We should pursue these good works, and by the grace of God we will receive the blessing."

2. REALIZE THAT THE SOURCE OF INJUSTICE IS OUR OWN DEPRAVITY. Dreams of an impartial, Utopian society fail to account for one crippling factor: human sin. The place to begin seeking global equality is within each individual. Christ's gospel, with its transforming power, remakes our minds and redirects our wills so that we renounce our selfish prejudices. Remember James' rebuke of the church:

> My brothers, show no partiality as you hold the faith of our Lord Jesus Christ, the Lord of glory. For if a man wearing a gold ring and fine clothing comes into your assembly, and a poor man in shabby clothing also comes in, and you pay attention to the one who wears the fine clothing . . . while you say to the poor man, "You stand over there," or "Sit down at my feet," have you not then . . . become judges with evil thoughts?

We are not living Christ's life when we favor the banker and put him on the church board just because of his status, yet neglect, often with some embarrassment, that needy family who can't afford trendy clothes and doesn't fit the profile of our targeted outreach group.

3. BE PATIENT IN EVALUATING PEOPLE AND WHAT THEY DO. Jesus cautions, "Do not judge by appearance, but judge with right judgment." Though first impressions are important, we sometimes write people off too hastily without allotting time for careful reflection. Hockey scouts told a young Wayne Gretzky he was too small and too slow for the National Hockey League. They missed it! He only became the greatest player in the sport's history.

4. WITH ALL YOUR BEST WILL, TRY TO TREAT PEOPLE FAIRLY. Recently I returned the now-defunct battery in my wife's car to the dealer where I had purchased it. The young attendant checked his records and told me the battery was five days *under* its three-year warranty. He treated me fairly when he could have hedged on the guarantee; I wouldn't have been the wiser since I didn't remember the exact purchase date. Echoing Job's square dealing with his servants, Paul tells "masters," or "employers," as we'd apply it today, to be fair to their workers since they too work for One who shows no partiality.

Extend the influence of Christ in your weekday world by treating all the people you know or meet with the courtesy you would like.

And while we're at it, all of us must repent and renounce any vestige of racial bias or social prejudice. Do it now.

5. DO WHAT YOU CAN TO PROMOTE RIGHTEOUSNESS AND JUSTICE IN SOCIETY. Remember that sin is both personal and social. It affects not only the person who commits it but also those around him. One of the reasons the state governs its citizens, according to Paul, is to be a "terror" and an "avenger" to those who disregard the well-being of the community. "The just purposes of human government include the commendation of good, the punishment of evil, the maintenance of peace, and the protection of the oppressed," argues J. Budziszewski. When public officials violate that God-ordained charge, they must be held to public accountability.

Christians must use the political process to whatever extent we can to advance justice in our culture. After all, we have dual citizenship, as Yancey reminds us:

> The world we live in is not an either/or world. What I do as a Christian—praying, worshiping, demonstrating God's love to the sick, needy, and imprisoned—is not exclusively supernatural or natural, but both working at the same time. Perhaps if Jesus stood in the flesh beside me, murmuring phrases like "I saw Satan fall" whenever I acted in His name, I would remember better the connections between the two worlds.

And Gil Bouton would be right: those old days would be gone forever.

CHAPTER 7

The Compassion Promise:

Job Resolves to Help Those in Need

Job 31:16–23, 31–32

If I have withheld anything that the poor desired,
or have caused the eyes of the widow to fail,
or have eaten my morsel alone,
and the fatherless has not eaten of it
(for from my youth the fatherless grew up with me as with a father,
and from my mother's womb I guided the widow),
if I have seen anyone perish for lack of clothing,
or the needy without covering,
if his body has not blessed me,
and if he was not warmed with the fleece of my sheep,
if I have raised my hand against the fatherless,
because I saw my help in the gate,
then let my shoulder blade fall from my shoulder,
and let my arm be broken from its socket.
For I was in terror of calamity from God,
and I could not have faced his majesty.

if the men of my tent have not said,
'Who is there that has not been filled with his meat?'
(the sojourner has not lodged in the street;
I have opened my doors to the traveler)

"But there will be no poor among you."—Moses

"For you always have the poor with you."—Jesus

So which is it? Moses envisions the Promised Land so overrun with blessings that no poverty exists. Fourteen centuries later Jesus states a simple fact of life in a destitute world. People with needs pass us on the street and live with us all the time. The difference is this: Moses spoke of what could and should be among the covenant people if they shared those blessings. Jesus gives us human reality. Yet with the reality comes an implicit challenge; we can do better. The truly poor are just trying to survive. Like it or not, their desperation is genuine.

Enter compassion, and where compassion meets desperation God's love blazes.

> Compassion asks us to go where it hurts, to enter places of pain, to share in brokenness, fear, confusion, and anguish. Compassion challenges us to cry out with those in misery, to mourn with those who are lonely, to weep with those in tears. Compassion requires us to be weak with the weak, vulnerable with the vulnerable, and powerless with the powerless. Compassion means full immersion into the condition of being human.

Job testifies that he has taken this plunge into compassion's depths.

WHAT JOB SAYS: WHAT'S MINE IS YOURS

Since no welfare state existed in the ancient Near East, people lacking life's basic necessities depended on the compassion of others. Sometimes the "haves" showed mercy and helped the "have nots"; sometimes they didn't. Job testifies that he had always provided for the needy when he had the opportunity. Earlier in the book, however, Eliphaz had claimed otherwise: "You (Job) . . . have withheld bread from the hungry . . . You have sent widows away empty, and the arms of the fatherless were crushed." Job later denied these charges: ". . . I delivered the poor who cried for help, and the fatherless who had none to help him . . . I caused the widow's heart to sing for joy . . . I was a father to the needy. . . ."

GIVE ME YOUR POOR

This line of defense now reaches its highest level here in Job's oath of innocence. In 31:16–23 and 31–32 he calls upon God to show him no mercy if he has shown none toward those who sought his help. Job begins his claim in verse 16 with a broad statement couched in another "if" clause, that he had not "withheld anything the poor desired." Though the word translated "poor" may refer only to those in financial straits, it usually speaks of poverty's effects within a culture, of vulnerable, exploited people, those "down and out." One special group of the disenfranchised were widows. Job had not "caused their eyes to fail"—that is he had never let them down when they had looked up to him for help.

Orphans, too, had enjoyed Job's gracious gifts. Verse 17 describes his willingness to share his food with them. While dining was a social function in the East, not every household would welcome guests when the meal was more modest. Yet a gracious spirit had characterized Job all of his life, according to verse 18. He had been like a father to orphans. When destitute children stood as potential victims in Job's community, this good man had refused to side with his influential friends against them. Widows knew his wise counsel advising them in the absence of their husbands. Fleece from his own sheep provided warm clothes for anyone facing death in the bitter night winds of the desert. For such generosity words of blessing had come Job's way from the lips of many a cold, hungry stranger.

He had welcomed them into his home, as was expected in a day when travelers depended on the hospitality of families along the route of their journey. That was who Job was and apparently everyone knew it. Verse 31 says that those who lived with him—

family and servants—talked about his penchant for lavishing the finest delicacies on his diners. He always put on quite a spread! "Who has not left his table filled?" they marveled among themselves, knowing the answer even before they asked. The stranger, or immigrant as we might say today, who had no place to stay was included at Job's table and invited to spend the night. Such an offer not only provided lodging but also protection. The "vacancy" sign was always out at Job's place.

WHEN GOD BREAKS YOUR ARM

Had this kind of integrity not marked his life, Job calls for God to bring judgment on him. Ironically, the imprecation described in verses 22 and 23 would render Job powerless to offer the very help he has just affirmed. He had used his arm, his strength, on behalf of the needy and had not "raised his hand" against them. Were that not true, Job petitions, let "my shoulder blade" detach from the joint and "let my arm be broken" at my elbow. God would thus destroy the arm that had "struck" the orphan and refused to help the widow.

Of course, that was not the case; and in verse 23 we learn one of the reasons for Job's compassionate favor toward the poor and oppressed. Of all things, it is his sense of God's justice which triggers Job's mercy. He was, as we recall, a man who feared God. He had also expressed amazement that his friends had shown little "terror" or "dread" in light of God's "majesty." Job, though, would not make that mistake. He had not used his lofty status among the townspeople as an excuse to mistreat them because he knew full well God's incomparable majesty over everyone and everything. His awareness of *Shaddai*'s majestic holiness compelled Job not to withdraw into an ivory-tower isolation or to lord it over others in a display of coercive authority, but to feed, counsel, clothe, support, shelter, and befriend them instead.

WHAT WE FACE: "PAUPERIZED HUMANITY"

"They're hypocrites, they don't care, they don't make a difference, they don't do anything." That's how one unbelieving educator described Christians. Alan Doswald had arranged to meet this professor for lunch in Fresno to discuss his claims. After the two exchanged comments for a few minutes, the skeptic

> . . . eventually admitted that no other group comes close to doing what Christians do to help others outside their circle. There is no Hindu homeless shelter in Fresno. There is no Buddhist food pantry in Fresno. There is no Muslim clothing ministry for street people in Fresno.

Even though the church doesn't do as well as we should in caring for the needy, God blesses the efforts of His children when they reach out to share His love with hurting people.

FEARS AND FRUSTRATIONS

Despite past successes, huge problems still impede the church's outreach. The volume and complexity of human need in our world today sometimes overwhelm the spirit. Some still see Walter Rauschenbusch's "social gospel" and its equation of social change with salvation behind Christian concern for physical needs. Others prefer to salve their conscience with the mistaken notion that the government's entitlement programs of doling out money indiscriminately—welfare—will take care of the problem.

To be sure, difficult issues frustrate our efforts to help; but so, too, do all sorts of small fears within every individual. I don't like for con artists to take advantage of me under the guise of seeking a handout. Several years ago as a young pastor I received a late night call from a stranger supposedly needing help. My well-meaning though naïve effort to respond soon put me in a situation where I was threatened with physical harm. I must admit that I was "gun shy" for a long time after that incident when it came to people's requests for material help. How foolish, I eventually realized, how unlike Jesus to allow petty self-will to prevent my obedience to Him and quell the joy that comes by serving others. I admit that I still struggle with that resistant spirit even though I know that God has called me to live, work, and serve among hurting, suffering people. After all, that's my own neighborhood, too.

ON SITE AND FACE-TO-FACE

So I take heart when I see Christians visit prisons to establish relationships with inmates or set up pregnancy care centers to give child care and adoption services as alternatives to abortion. Gospel outreaches also fund shelters for abused women and children as well as orphanages and schools. Bob Lupton's *FCS Urban Ministries* organization and others like it build houses at low cost for high risk families. So many of the elderly, disabled, and homebound—those in "distressing disguise"—need caregivers who will touch them with Christ's compassion by feeding, bathing, clothing, and sitting with them as caring companions. We fill these gaps not just by sending money, but by being on-site, face-to-face with people at the point of their need.

The ghastly aftermath of Hurricane Katrina along the Gulf coast in 2005 saw Christians rolling up their sleeves to help as never before. Tens of thousands of volunteers from churches in every corner of the nation sped to New Orleans and Pass Christian and Gulfport where they cleaned up debris, repaired homes, treated injuries, and fed the starving. Said Frederick Turner, "In hours (after Katrina) whole organizations had sprung into being, anchored on churches and other moral institutions of civil society. . . ." So too Christ's arms reach out through his people to AIDS patients in South Africa, Zambia, and Namibia; to earthquake and tsunami victims in Afghanistan, Pakistan, Indonesia, Japan and Haiti.

As Doswald notes, "God owns the biggest business in town." His church "is full of people who are ready to make a difference through service. They have the gifts needed, and there is work for them to do. All that remains is mobilization." Much of that work is the unseen, "cup of cold water" kind that happens in dark, dirty places never to be featured in glossy, four-color poster spreads. Yet this is Christ's body living His values in a desperate world. John Weaver, the last American aid worker to leave Afghanistan after 9/11, returned to that war-shredded land to share the compassion of Jesus with people racked by war, death, and misery. "I have stacked, carried, and distributed a literal mountain of wheat in Afghanistan that was grown in my homeland," he reflects. "We will continue to focus on rebuilding-life issues, because we know this results in reigniting hopes, refueling dreams, restarting relationships, and regaining joy and purpose for life." We *do* care, we *do* make a difference, and we *must* do what we can.

WHAT WE MUST DO: SERVE THE BREAD OF LIFE

Peter's words sound like a job listing in the classifieds for a "servant": ". . . (H)ave unity of mind, sympathy, brotherly love, a tender heart, and a humble mind." To have a chance at landing that position, what should we do? Here are some places to start.

1. STOP WAITING FOR A "FEELING" OF COMPASSION TO COME OVER YOU. We don't need an emotional high when we already have a clear command from the Lord: "Love your neighbor." What He expects is obedience, not a mood swing. Don't delay until the spirit moves you toward a frame of mind to help; instead, move yourself toward the first person you see who needs help. Christ has the authority to mandate compassion. True love as the Bible depicts it is a choice, an act of the will to give and may not immediately be "felt" or evident. What's more, love is personal. As Yancey says, institutions can't love. Only people love.

2. DON'T LET THE GLUT OF INFORMATION ABOUT THE NEEDY HARDEN YOU. Everywhere we turn the images are in our face. Newscasts, infomercials, the Internet, documentaries, and mail appeals overload our senses with scenes of the starving, the homeless, the diseased, and the dying. It's easy to become calloused, to click the remote, throw up our hands, and turn our eyes away. Our response amounts to, "I'm only one person and there's nothing I can do about all this," so we do nothing. That's exactly what we must *not* do. Our sense of people's hurt must have a single face in view. Look to one individual rather than at the anonymous masses in the Sudan or Uzbekistan. Find the appropriate avenues in your church or the agencies in your town that can help you personally look into the eyes of one hurting person who needs someone—who needs you—to care.

3. MEET LITTLE NEEDS AROUND YOU FIRST. Personally I don't know anyone like Warren Buffet who can leave billions of dollars to charity or like artists who stage concerts such as the Live 8 series for African relief. What I do have, though, is the gift of community, a circle of faith relationships with people I know. Many of those I love in that circle lack a family support system since ours is a fragmented, transient culture. Within my Christian community I bump into needs that I can help meet. If we can't or won't help the people we see all the time, we probably won't reach out to those we never see. The early church modeled this *koinonia* compassion when they gave what they had as individuals needed it.

4. QUIT WORRYING SO MUCH ABOUT "CLOCK TIME." We obey the orders of our smart phones and PDAs, shuttling to and from meetings and appointments, blind to everything around us except deadlines and bottom lines. Helping people, though—*really* helping people—will move us from "clock time" to "taking time." Prepare to be interrupted, put upon, postponed, detained, and delayed—in other words, having compassion means having time and being "displaced." How contradictory it seems that in a day of unprecedented moving, relocating, and transitioning for employment and career, God's people are less willing than ever to pull up stakes, leave home, and sacrifice when He calls us to go to the hurting.

5. LEARN TO SEE THE CHRISTIAN LIFE AS OF ONE PIECE, NOT MANY PIECES. Our experience of redemption is not salvation *plus* service and other "extras." Paul says that when we received mercy, ministry came with it. It's a package deal. Compassionate service grows out of our new birth experience, not as something tacked on but as a built-in component that enriches and deepens our lives as we mature in Christ. The longer we walk with Him in grace the more effective our service for Him should be. After all, when He saved us God had already arranged for us to leave a trail of good works. It's like a good marriage. I'm in love with the same woman I pledged myself to over thirty years ago. But over time I find new dimensions of this amazing person I love and new ways of showing my love for her.

6. GLADLY EMBRACE SERVICE AS A SPIRITUAL DISCIPLINE. Prayer, Bible intake, meditation, worship, and service are some of the "exercises that help us train for godliness." The more we give ourselves to serve the needy the more we discover our own need, our spiritual poverty and total dependence on God. A regimen of serving also furthers God's work of shaping Christ-likeness in us. Jesus "went about doing good." As Brennan Manning comments, "There was a towering desire within Jesus to reveal His Father in serving the poor, the captive, the blind, and all who were in need." As we follow Christ's example of service we reveal Him to those we serve.

7. TAKE A BOLD STEP TO PRACTICE HOSPITALITY. Volunteer to house the next missionary family that visits your church. "To invite people into our homes is to respond with gratitude to the God who made a home for us," Winner suggests. Bobby was a layman in our church who was so burdened for Herman, a homeless alcoholic in the community, that he invited Herman to live with him, his wife, and two daughters until he could find permanent housing. During the weeks he stayed with Bobby's family, Herman saw the gospel of Jesus lived out in little ways every day. The gospel put food on the table before him. The gospel turned down the blanket on a warm bed for him and eased him back into a La-Z-Boy around a family circle that had expanded so he could fit inside. The loving hospitality of Bobby's family and their humble, sacrificial self-giving impacted this lonely man in such a way that he came to trust Christ. We must make room in our lives for people who have nowhere else to turn.

8. AS YOU SHARE WHAT YOU HAVE, ALWAYS SHARE WHO CHRIST IS. To be sure, loving people through Christ means we show concern for their physical needs. To offer them the gospel only to turn away from their material poverty betrays a coldness foreign to His compassionate heart. But as the top priority, we must offer them the gospel! These are our marching orders: to make disciples as we go about our lives. Christ came to seek and to save those lost in sin, wandering from God, and hungry for eternal life. When Laura Belle Barnard left South Georgia to serve in India over seventy years ago, here's what she encountered:

> In the bazaar where one must shop, I was literally besieged by licensed paupers who knew nothing but to beg . . . The unkempt and matted hair, the filthy skin, and ragged clothing, if any, all presented a most repulsive sight . . . They grope and reach out, unconsciously I believe, for the Bread of Life.

Let's be sure they have this Bread to eat.

CHAPTER 8

The Worship Promise:

Job Resolves to Be Devoted to God

Job 31:26–28

If I have looked at the sun when it shone,
or the moon moving in splendor,
and my heart has been secretly enticed,
and my mouth has kissed my hand,
this also would be an iniquity to be punished by the judges,
for I would have been false to God above.

Hero worship—I had a bad case of it. When I was a boy, every time I'd see my grandfather he'd needle me. "Your buddy Mickey Mantle and his Yankees aren't doing so hot, are they? Don't think they're gonna make it to the Series this year!" He and I didn't exactly see eye-to-eye when it came to Mantle and the Yanks. He hated them. Me, I idolized the Mick and his team. I really think my affection for number seven would have rivaled Billy Crystal's. I knew Mickey's life story—all about his humble beginnings as Mutt Mantle's son from the northeast Oklahoma mining country. Year by year I kept up with his stats and could recite on command all manner of Mantle trivia: his 565-foot home run on April 17, 1953, at Griffith Stadium in Washington, still the longest regular season four-bagger officially on record, and that's just one example among thousands of bits of data I had stored away in my Mantle-crazed brain.

In the early 1960s I didn't know of any such thing as licensed clothing with official team logos, so I bought a plain black cap and painted a white "NY" Yankee logo on it. I did the same with a black magic marker on a white t-shirt, adding a big "seven"—Mantle's number—on the back. When I started playing Little League baseball I had to have uniform number seven. My coach, Gaither Maddox, liked me so he obliged. Standing at the plate I'd emulate the Mick's waggle with the bat, and whenever I could I'd trot with the same gait he had.

The year before he retired, Mantle came to my hometown for a speaking engagement. I was at the front of the line but he walked right past me; I was so awestruck that I couldn't get out the words to ask for his autograph. A policeman got it for me later that night, and to this day I have an autographed picture of Mickey Mantle in my office. More than anyone or anything else, my infatuation with this hero drove me to play baseball. I read his book, *The Quality of Courage*, and wanted to hit, run, and throw like he did. In later years I came to realize that like all of us and the "idols" we set before us, Mantle was a weak and flawed man. When he died, though, I cried.

We long to give ourselves with the highest pitch of passion to someone or something we admire. Job confronts this question of ultimate devotion and testifies that his allegiance belongs to the One who alone is worthy of it. He had "turned to God from idols to serve the true and living God."

WHAT JOB SAYS: DEEPLY DEVOTED AT THE DEEPEST LEVEL

This section, verses 26-28, presents the most unusual condition in Job's oath. All of the others involve his ethical conduct—matters regarding women, truth-telling, justice, wealth, the land, and so forth. Here, however, he addresses the supreme issue in life: complete devotion to God. Integrity always involves what a person believes at the heart's deepest level and how these ultimate core principles shape behavior. Despite the prevalent worship of multiple gods throughout ancient Near Eastern culture, including Edom where Job likely lived, this man of integrity had remained loyal to the only true God who is totally distinct from the world He created.

Little information about the religion of Edom has survived from antiquity, so we're mostly in the dark about specific beliefs and rituals which Job's neighbors might have practiced. Based on inscriptions we do have, Edomites apparently worshiped a god named Qos, or Quas/Koze, as he is also called. The meaning of his name may associate him with weather, perhaps as a storm god; however no evidence connects him with the sun. Regardless, Job is well aware of sun worship.

FALSE LIGHT IN EDEN'S SHADOWS

Job's statements in this section move along familiar paths. Like Eve's seduction by the serpent in Eden, his denial begins with the consideration of a "look," a glance toward the illicit object. He then moves to the possibility that the object might allure him with its appeal. The final step envisions his devotion to the fetish. In the same way, Eve "saw," "desired," then "took." Had Job turned from the true God to venerate creation instead, he would have committed monstrous sin.

The context begun in verses 24 and 25 continues in verse 26. Under discussion are issues of "trust" and "confidence"—concerns of worship, in other words. Job has never idolized gold, he has said; now he vows that the sun and moon have never lured his affections away from the God who made them. The word used here for "sun" emphasizes its brightness and brilliance from an earth-centered point of view. Its evening consort, the moon, shines in radiant "splendor" as Job pictures its stately glide across the night sky. He may be describing the silver sheen of the full moon or, as Hippolyta recites in *A Midsummer Night's Dream*, a new moon "like to a silver bow new-bent in heaven."

Job has not given in to the seductive appeal of this idolatrous worship of nature. These luminaries had failed to "entice" his heart in secret. To "entice" in Hebrew carries the idea of leading someone astray due to that person's naïveté. It describes Delilah's attempts to seduce Samson; Job uses the word in verse nine the same way. A most relevant warning from Yahweh in Deuteronomy uses the same term translated "deceive": "Take care lest your heart be deceived, and you turn aside and serve other gods and worship them." Had he fallen prey to this danger, Job's "worship of God would have been hypocrisy" for he would have "disowned in secret the God whom he acknowledged openly and outwardly." The worship of any part of creation is false and involves deception by its very nature because the created order is *not* the ultimate reality of the universe. As Creator, God alone is.

A KISS BEFORE DYING

Although devotion to God originates as heart loyalty, it necessarily shows up in one's conduct. We act as a result of who we are. Job had never "thrown a kiss" to the sun and moon as a sign of his affection for them. Pliny alludes to this practice of blowing a kiss to deity, as do Tacitus and Lucian. The Lord commends the seven thousand in Israel who had not "kissed" Baal. Hosea describes eighth century B. C. idolaters in Israel this way: "Those who offer human sacrifices kiss calves," referring to the calf-shaped idols they had crafted. Ironically the only time Job does bring his hand to his mouth is when he falls broken and contrite before Yahweh. "Behold, I am of small account," he laments. "I have spoken once, and I will not answer; twice, but I will proceed no further." With this hand-to-mouth gesture he respects rather than renounces the Lord.

Had Job given his allegiance to another as deity, he would have committed "great iniquity," according to verse 28. The Old Testament contains an extensive vocabulary for breaching God's holiness; sin, transgression, rebellion, evil, wickedness, unfaithfulness, and treachery are among the most serious violations.

"Iniquity" fits right in with this class. The Semitic source of this word has to do with that which is bent, twisted, or crooked. It may refer to an actual deed, as it does here, or to an awareness of guilt produced by the wrongful act, or to the punishment the guilty deed merits. Only God, not the solar systems He made, deserves worship since He is "above" them.

WHAT WE FACE: AMERICAN IDOLS

Even in today's secular, techno-driven, third millennium world, worship is a huge topic for all of us. Some people would never admit as much, but the truth is that every person is a worshiper. We can't help it. It's built into our nature. Even the most ardent atheist bows before some "altar." Most often the god of self—self-will and self-sufficiency—receives his adoration. He may or may not admit that this is so. Actually however, his denial is itself part of his egotistical worship since it represents an attempt to lend respectability to his massive stock of pride.

"A GOD BEGOTTEN IN THE SHADOWS OF A FALLEN HEART"

We err if we think that nature worship was limited to a pre-modern view of the world. Job's recognition that some people blow kisses to the sun parallels many non-Christian beliefs in 21st century pop culture. Much of this celebrity pantheism in America traces back to the 1800s and the transcendental philosophy promoted by such writers as Emerson and Thoreau. Their concept was that God, the "Oversoul," exists within every part of nature and offers each person "rebirth" as they reject society's norms and traditions to live by intuition and instinct. Modern interest in nature worship owes its popularity to an influx of similar Eastern pantheistic religion. Marketed by such celebrities as Richard Gere, Shirley MacLaine, Keanu Reeves, Uma Thurman, and others, Yoga and Zen meditation spread Buddhism's teachings to the suburbs. Fascination with pagan religion continues to grow as America increasingly spurns its Judeo-Christian roots.

DO WE SING THE DOXOLOGY OR "DRAW ME CLOSE?"

Among evangelical Christians who embrace these roots, worship-related issues stir controversy. Few among God's people would deny the necessity of worship or debate the essence of what it is. Yet opinions differ over styles and forms of worship. For convenience let's summarize the dispute by focusing on two poles of tension inherent to the nature of worship itself. Some worship tends toward what I'll call an *objective* expression of worship: truth, the mind, reason, content, and tradition. This view of worship tends toward the liturgical, sees God as exalted, and emphasizes formal routines of discipline and aesthetic beauty in honoring and exalting the fear of God.

The more *subjective* dynamic in worship seeks to engage the heart and the spirit primarily. Its concerns include feeling and intimacy with God, freedom and emotion in worship style, as well as innovation and a sense of wonder at the love of God. If this approach provides the heart in worship, the first supplies light. In the more formal service, worshipers sitting in a Gothic-style sanctuary might hear Handel's *Arioso* as a prelude, recite the Apostles' Creed, hear an exposition of Ephesians 4, and sing *Gloria Patri* as benediction. Participants in the more relaxed setting encircle the platform in a theatre-in-the-round arrangement, some standing and some sitting, listening to a 45-minute set by the praise band which includes covering a Switchfoot number, praying spontaneously from the floor, viewing a video clip from the movie *The Blind Side*, and hearing a message entitled, "Cell-Phone Evangelism and Other Hang-Ups." Alan Wolfe, in his landmark study of how religion in the United States "is being transformed in radically new directions," contends that in recent years the pendulum has swung to these latter informal, need-driven forms of worship which offer little "otherworldly reverence."

HEART, SOUL, MIND, AND STRENGTH

While his diagnosis is almost certainly correct, we are currently seeing a corrective response with more focus on content and a vertical view of God's transcendence in worship. Such a recovery is vital because both head and heart comprise authentic worship. Our devotion to God must engage the mind with doctrinal truth because we can't worship Him if we don't know Him as He really is. "The idolatrous heart assumes that God is other than He is . . . and substitutes for the true God one made after its own likeness," A. W. Tozer argues. Scripture must fill our preaching, teaching, reading, praying, and singing or we risk the abomination of false worship.

At the same time worship that presses to know God truly will always lead us through vistas that give glimpses of the Most High God in all His magnificence and leave us amazed in "astonished reverence"—"captivated, charmed, and entranced," as Tozer puts it. The living God is always beyond our comprehension. In the sacred page but beyond as well, in holy places deep within our lives, we fall before the God whose "splendor covered the heavens," says Habakkuk as he glimpsed the "brightness" of the Holy One. Even this spectacular display, the prophet realizes, is but a "veiled" hint of the Lord's undiluted power.

When we participate in worship's mystery, we come away with an awakened sense of how desperately we need God and of our guilt before Him. Too much of what passes for worship today reflects nothing more than our own "designer religion" tailored to our own attempts at manipulating God for our purposes. The contrite worshiper bends the knee to the fear of God instead, celebrating divine goodness, yes, but always with a tearful heart lamenting his own sin. Ironically this dread of a holy God's wrath compels us to a closer intimacy with Him. Fear and love are never in conflict when we approach God's throne in sincere humility and trust. As the psalmist beautifully puts it, "But with you there is forgiveness, that you may be feared." Mercy and truth kiss one another as we worship the Christ who is both God's righteousness and redemption winged into our hearts.

Therefore any supposed worship which neglects Christ's gospel and salvation is untrue. Eugene Peterson reminds us that salvation must eventually turn into worship otherwise it diminishes the gospel to nothing more than a concept and a technique we can manipulate. God's larger purpose in the gospel is to "restore the missing jewel" of worship "that we might . . . learn to do again what we were created to do in the first place—worship the Lord in the beauty of holiness . . . ." Worship thus celebrates, proclaims, and magnifies the gospel of Christ's redeeming grace that reconciles us to God. What we must seek, then, is that total-personality worship of God that hungers to know Him truly and supremely. With that knowledge comes the most intense feeling we can know because it leads to a God-saturated life abandoned to love Him without reserve.

WHAT WE MUST DO: SWIM IN THE SUNBEAM

It's true that we can't reduce worship to a formula, as if to say, "Do this then add that and you'll worship God properly." Much of what happens when we meet the living God is unscripted. But we can better prepare ourselves for our appointments with Him.

1. ALWAYS APPROACH GOD AS ULTIMATE, NEVER AS A MEANS TO HELP YOU ACHIEVE YOUR OWN AGENDA. In our secular culture "self" is sovereign. Even the religious world has recast God so that we will feel at home with Him. He is our "need-meeter." We give Him a "to do" list, but He'd better not make many demands of us. God is now, in effect, a means to help us get what we want: a new image, success, wealth, self-confidence, and on it goes. You've seen the ads and heard the testimonials. Yet God is who He says He is, not what I want Him to be for me. I come to Him solely on His terms. He is ultimate and final, never a means to an end. We commit the highest treason when we try to turn God into a psycho-soothing, feel-good errand boy who will cater to our selfish whims.

2. SCRIPTURE MUST GOVERN OUR WORSHIP. Our celebration of God must involve more than a thin veneer of theology; biblical truth is the DNA of worship. Since God reveals Himself in His word, anything in our service to Him that violates Scripture dishonors Him. Revealed truth always sits in judgment on our up and down, inconsistent feelings. So we always worship within a context, whether publicly or in private. By that I mean that even though we are individuals and express our uniqueness in our worship, we must guard against "homemade belief" or maverick worship. Such an attitude tends toward pride and isolation. The Bible, our faith community, and church history and tradition help to shape our approach and response to God.

3. DON'T BE AFRAID OF DEEP FEELING AND EMOTION IN WORSHIP. One problem with our age is that it's not cool to be extreme about religion, even among religious people. Yet when we realize who God is, see Him in the beauty of holiness, understand the tragedy of our sin, and receive His gracious forgiveness, we will delight in Him passionately, sing for Him with zeal, pray to Him fervently, and obey Him with an excited, adoring heart. Find out what pleases God, then do it with passion. When you do, you're in the middle of worship. Experience and emotion do not displace truth, but loving truth always forges deeply-held conviction laced with emotion. That's total personality worship.

4. REVISIT YOUR FEAR OF THE LORD. Though it sounds strange, the greater our fear of God the closer we feel to Him. Any notion of Him as "the man upstairs" or "the big guy" is false and unworthy of God. The only way to be intimate with the Lord is to know Him as He really is. When we bow to His infinite greatness, He draws us to that place near His heart. There's no need for us to try to reduce the distance. He'll do that as we exalt Him. Remember, "The friendship of the LORD is for those who fear him." As you worship by reading His word and communing with Him, pause to reflect on His beauty, His wisdom, His glory. Take time to adore the Lord before you ask Him for something.

5. WORK HARD TO REMEMBER THAT WORSHIP IS A WAY OF LIFE. Worship is not just something we do on Sunday in a building; it's who we are 24/7. In recent years many have tended to equate worship primarily with music. Somehow we've bought into America's fascination with celebrity and performance, so we sit in the pew while the singers and instrumentalists entertain—er, I mean, minister to us. In true worship, though, God is the audience and all of us participate by offering Him all that His worth demands. Our sacrifice of praise calls for excellence in all that we do to honor God, whether it's making beautiful music, praying alone in silence, or reading the holy text. Our hearts must desire only to express God's unsearchable glory with the best effort we can give. Yet the reach of worship is longer still, extending beyond the building where we meet on Sundays. If we can glorify God by what we eat and drink and by what we do with our bodies, then it is a matter of worship as to whether we honor Him by the words we use when our guard is down, the places we go when we want to have fun, and the friends we hang with when we want to belong.

6. WORSHIP ALWAYS INVOLVES THE CHOICES WE MAKE. "All worship is prerogative," as George Herbert remarks. God invites us to rejoice in Him, but He never coerces or forces us to comply. We will not reverence Him, however, unless our hearts overflow with gratitude to Him. Only then will we worship sincerely, putting aside pretense. Some believers feel comfortable with liturgy and formal structure in corporate worship; others benefit from more freedom and a relaxed atmosphere. In whatever way we honor the Lord, worship should be "our normal enjoyment." N. T. Wright concludes, "When we begin to glimpse the reality of God, the natural reaction is to worship him." The key is to keep the fire of daily intimacy with God blazing in our hearts. If we fill our thoughts and affections with Him, then we'll worship as we ought.

In a Sunday communion sermon over 160 years ago, Robert Murray McCheyne spoke from Hosea's prophecy:

> . . . (Y)ou have access to Him who is the fountain of happiness, of peace, of holiness—what have you to do any more with idols? Oh, if your heart swims in the rays of God's love, like a little mote swimming in the sunbeam, you will have no room in your heart for idols.

CHAPTER 9

The Forgiveness Promise:

Job Resolves to Be Merciful to His Enemies

Job 31:29–30

If I have rejoiced at the ruin of him who hated me,
or exulted when evil overtook him
(I have not let my mouth sin
by asking for his life with a curse),

"I'm gonna get you, Junior Barnes." Bill Cosby's old stand-up routine entitled "Revenge" tells of a snowball fight when he was a kid. Cosby's pal, Junior Barnes, hit him with an illegal missile: a slushball with a rock packed inside. From that day, Cosby plotted to get even. According to his plan, he fashioned the perfect snowball—perfectly round and smooth—and put it in the kitchen freezer until the time was right. July—the hot summer had arrived. Time for revenge. As Junior Barnes played on Cosby's front porch one random afternoon, unsuspecting of the danger that lurked just inside, the avenger set his plan into motion. With subdued glee so as not to arouse suspicion, he went inside to retrieve the weapon and execute the plot—until he realized, when he searched the freezer, that his mother had thrown the snowball away. So he went outside and spit on Junior Barnes instead!

Sweet revenge. The "eye for an eye" instinct is so deeply rooted in our nature that it seems impossible to try to overcome it. When Laura Blumenfeld sought counsel as she tried to forgive the man who had shot her father, the priest told her of Jesus' forgiveness of His enemies. "It's in line with my faith," he conceded, "but it goes against my grain as a human being." Through history, from Lamech's first bragging song about revenge, people have "gotten even."

Our insistence on settling the score is so much a part of us that we wonder if we hear Job right. The good will he offers the enemy here is his most audacious claim yet. Bernhard Duhm puts it like this: "If chapter 31 is the crown of all the ethical development of the Old Testament, verse 29 is the jewel of that crown."

WHAT JOB SAYS: NO HARD FEELINGS

The wasted figure must have thought about it many times during his exile to the ash pile. "What do the townspeople think of me now? Are they looking at me the same way Eliphaz, Bildad, and Zophar are, wondering what terrible thing I have done?" Job tried to recall those people he might have offended. "Is there someone I mistreated—a business associate, an employee, a guest? Did I shortchange a partner by mistake or make an off-the-cuff remark he might have taken the wrong way? Is he now thinking that I'm getting what I deserve?"

"I HATE ASPARAGUS"

In verses 29 and 30, Job vows to God that he has not treated *his* enemies that way. He issues three denials, the first two in parallel statements and a third so bold that even considering such an action should shock us. Job contends that there is no way "I have rejoiced at the ruin of him who hated me, or exulted when evil overtook him . . . ." It's hard to imagine who might have "hated" this good man, but keep in mind that the Hebrew word for "hate" carries a wide range of meaning. For example, there's a big difference when we say "I hate asparagus" and "I hate my neighbor," but this term in Job's language could cover both extremes and everything in the middle.

Job may have even had his friends in mind. After all, they were accusing him of sin. In a sense, they had done to him the very thing he is denying. They claim he is suffering because of what he's done wrong. The three of them gloat, "We're right about you, Job. We know the truth. Your pain proves our case." These "friends" were "exulting" over Job's calamity because in their minds, it proved their argument. We can almost hear the smugness when Eliphaz asserts, "Yes, this is the way things are." Zophar is even more snobbish. "How dare you insult my intelligence like this!" he lashes back at Job. Others in town may have despised Job or resented his status and wealth.

Then when ruin had come their way, no gleeful shout had come from Job's lips. The word "evil" often has the idea in the Old Testament of trouble or misfortune without a moral connotation. When hard times had blitzed an enemy's house, Job did not "rejoice." This verb and its companion, "exult," express total joy. People "rejoice" over salvation, their children, good things, the law, their work, festival days, and the Lord Himself, according to the Hebrew Scriptures. Job had sung no such song over a foe's misery.

What's more, Job had certainly not invoked a curse asking God to take someone's life. Though many ancient cultures practiced such extreme measures of vengeance, Job recognizes that such a prayer would be sinful. He had turned neither his heart nor his voice against anyone who had opposed him.

BUT IS JOB CONSISTENT?

Two questions arise in light of Job's testimony, however. First, does he really believe in the concept of justice? Should those who do wrong receive punishment for their crimes, or does Job's refusal to rejoice over an enemy's trouble signal that he is "soft" on this issue? For an answer, all we need to do is look at what he has already said. God is "angry" with those who sin, Job acknowledges, and He "puts out the lamp" of the wicked. Their "heritage" from the Lord is often hunger, pestilence, and loss, as "terrors overtake him like a flood." Job's firm avowal of righteous justice makes his gracious spirit of forgiveness all the more amazing.

What about these comments he makes in chapter 27, though? "Let my enemy be as the wicked, and let him who rises up against me be as the unrighteous. For what is the hope of the godless when God cuts him off, when God takes away his life?" Don't these sentiments contradict what Job says about not delighting in an enemy's fall? When we read the two passages closely, we observe that his oath in chapter 31 denies any notion of "getting even" personally on Job's part. Chapter 27, on the other hand, verifies divine judgment upon the "godless" as fact: "God will cut him off." Job is identifying his enemies as *God's* enemies. "I'm still holding to my righteousness," Job asserts, "and anyone who says otherwise shows his own wickedness—and I know that God's judgment awaits the wicked." In essence he's saying, "It takes one to know one. These people do not recognize my righteousness, so they must not be righteous." Job's claim still holds. He had not wished harm on those who had done so to him.

WHAT WE FACE: "REVENGE IS SWEET"

"The literary and religious story of Western culture is, in large measure, the tale of vengeance," claims Peter French. If you check out the films we watch, the books we read, and the songs we hear, you'll have to agree he has a point. Standing on the Coliseum floor in *Gladiator*, General Maximus tells the cowardly Commodus, "I will have my revenge" for the murder of his family. Westerns especially lend themselves to the revenge genre, whether it's *Shane*, the preacher in *Pale Rider*, Ethan Edwards in *The Searchers*, or Mattie Ross in *True Grit*. "I'm here to kill you, Little Bill, for what you did to Ned," vows William Munny, Clint Eastwood's character in *Unforgiven*.

The motive to "get even" flourishes in literature as well. Over half of Homer's *Iliad* traces Achilles' quest for vengeance upon Agamemnon and Hector. In fact, this lust for blood payment underlies much of Greek mythology. Shakespeare takes up the theme as well. In response to the promptings of his father's ghost to bring vengeance on Claudius, Hamlet reluctantly accepts his role as avenger: "The time is out of joint. O cursed spite, that ever I was born to set it right!" He later concedes, ". . . the croaking raven doth bellow for revenge." Poe's *The Cask of Amontillado* finds Montresor taking his grisly revenge upon Fortunato by burying the old man alive. I must admit, too, that when I first read Agatha Christie's *Murder on the Orient Express*, the resolution of the mystery gave me a satisfying sense of "you asked for it, you got it."

On a day-to-day level, who isn't outraged over a senseless killing reported on the evening news, and more than a little sympathetic when the victim's family cries out for vengeance in justice? When a co-worker tells lies about us, it seems natural to want to get even for what she's done. One variation on the golden rule for our age is, "Do unto others because they have done unto you."

"THE SOFTER PILLOW"

While much of twenty-first century culture sanctions this "eye for an eye" approach to moral authority, other voices in society lobby for compassion. Today's moral philosophers thus part company when it comes to the issue of "sweet revenge." Those who defend the place of personal vengeance argue that it is essential to a moral community. By nature we have this "primitive sense of the just" which responds to our basic "moral emotions" of resentment and indignation when someone injures us. Revenge, they say, provides us with a sense of vindication, a "moral empowerment" in which we act to defend our honor and maintain our self-respect. Any notion of forgiving or overlooking a personal wrong weakens the moral foundation of our culture, some argue, by promoting a "victimization" mentality. Loving our enemies makes for a "pretty clumsy moral philosophy," Michael Moore suggests.

Recently, however, in contrast to those who justify the role of vengeance in society, many psychologists have promoted the value of "interpersonal forgiveness." They point to the powerful therapeutic role of compassion, love, and benevolence toward those who offend us. We can avoid symptoms of distress and depression by exercising our wills to choose forgiveness, to abandon anger, and to respond to the offender in a loving way. Studies show that forgiveness, not vengeance, promotes increased self-esteem and self-respect. Human experience, both in real life and in fiction, testifies to the moral worth of forgiveness. People of integrity forgive. In *Les Miserables*, Father Myriel's stunning pardon of Jean Valjean transforms the ex-convict into a man of compassion and tenderness.

Emily and Katie Benton entered London's underground tube on July 7, 2005 as excited tourists out to see the city. Minutes later shrapnel and smoke engulfed them when a terrorist's bomb exploded in their subway car. Though they survived the blast, both suffered serious injuries. Katie thought she had been buried alive, she said. Their parents, Dudley and Patty Benton, issued this remarkable statement about their daughters' horrific experience: "We need to forgive the people who have done this to them," citing the danger of holding anger in their hearts. Job knew this danger as well.

WHAT WE MUST DO: STOP THE CYCLE

Forgiving a person who wrongs us flies in the face of our nature and our culture. Though it often takes a massive struggle to yield our wills to the Spirit, we can overcome a vengeful mindset. The road to a forgiving spirit, though long and often uphill, is open to traffic. Here are ways to begin the trip.

1. SEE PERSONAL RETALIATION FOR THE SIN IT REALLY IS. Don't let yourself off the hook. We become guilty when we return evil for evil. Bitterness and an unforgiving spirit poison all of life. When we hold a grudge, the grudge actually holds us. Chrysostom advises, "Let us not thrust the sword into ourselves by being revengeful."

2. AT THE DEEPEST LEVELS OF YOUR WILL, SUBMIT YOUR DESIRE FOR VENGEANCE TO CHRIST AND LET HIM DEAL WITH IT. Do we really believe that only an all-knowing, impartial, holy God has the ultimate right to enforce justice as He sees it? If so, revenge is none of our business. We have no jurisdiction here. Let the proper authority handle it.

3. BE CONVINCED OF THE BENEFIT AND BLESSING THAT COME TO YOUR LIFE WHEN YOU FORGIVE OTHERS. We can't control how others respond to our forgiveness, but we can, as Yancey says, "halt the cycle of blame and pain, breaking the chain of ungrace" in *our* experience. Refuse to live as a prisoner of bitterness. "Forgive one another, as God in Christ forgave you."

4. LIVE AGAPĒ LOVE. The New Covenant love Christ has dispersed throughout our hearts is a selfless, giving surrender of ego gratification. It calls us to reach out to love and serve others. As Leon Morris describes it, this is "love even of the unworthy, love which is not drawn out by merit in the beloved but which proceeds from the fact that the lover chooses to be a loving person." The character of God lives through us when we love the unlovely. "Christ says in effect, 'Your love must become such that you will no longer be governed and controlled by what people say. Your life must be governed by a new principle in yourself, a new principle of love,'" contends D. Martyn Lloyd-Jones.

5. LOVE JUSTICE, BUT SUBMIT TO GOD'S DESIGN FOR IMPLEMENTING IT. The "eye for an eye" code of justice described in the Torah belongs to civil magistrates. God never intended that individuals use it as a personal warrant authorizing vigilante vengeance. Those who follow Job's example can love both forgiveness and justice. One does not exclude the other.

6. WHEN WE FORGIVE, WE ACKNOWLEDGE OUR NEED FOR FORGIVENESS. Humility and a gracious spirit fit hand-in-glove. As we forgive others, our own sin becomes more apparent—but so does God's great love in taking it away. "Repay no one evil for evil," Paul commands. Instead, "outdo one another in showing honor."

7. REMIND YOURSELF THAT FORGIVENESS OPENS THE DOOR TO MINISTRY OPPORTUNITIES. Elisabeth Elliot's husband Jim was one of five pioneer missionaries killed by the Waorani people in 1956 along the Curaray River in Ecuador. Yet she and the other widows returned to share the gospel with her husband's killers. Christ used her forgiveness as a prelude to His. We can't risk closing the door to someone's spirit because we won't let go of our petty grudges.

8. THE FIRST PLACE TO PRACTICE FORGIVENESS IS WITH THE PEOPLE WE LOVE THE MOST. If someone you love has wronged you, let that love, not revenge, control how you respond to them. Don't allow the injury you have suffered to shape your spirit toward that person. The New Testament word used most often for forgiveness literally means "a putting off" or "sending away." Bishop Handley Moule urges, "In Christ find possible the impossible; let the resentment of nature die, at His feet, in the breath of His love."

Come before the Lord's throne often with Christina Rossetti's prayer:

> O Lord Jesus, because, being surrounded with infirmities we often sin and have to ask pardon, help us to forgive as we would be forgiven; neither mentioning old offenses committed against us, nor dwelling upon them in thought, nor being influenced by them in heart; but loving our brother freely, as you have loved us. For your name's sake.

CHAPTER 10

The Confession Promise:

Job Resolves to Be Open about His Sin

Job 31:33–34

If I have concealed my transgressions as others do
by hiding my iniquity in my bosom,
because I stood in great fear of the multitude,
and the contempt of families terrified me,
so that I kept silence, and did not go out of doors—

Clark Kent and Superman, identical? A "mild-mannered reporter" and this "strange visitor from another planet . . . with powers and abilities far beyond those of mortal men" the same person? No way—but, could it be? In the movie *Superman Returns*, cub reporter Jimmy Olsen begins to wonder when the Man of Steel and Mr. Kent return from long absences at the very same time. I remember from the old *Adventures of Superman* television series that Lois Lane often suspected Clark of leading a double life. She and Jimmy almost uncovered his secret identity several times—almost! Whew!

Job had no secret identity. What you saw of him—in the city gate, on his knees for his children, or languishing on the ash pile—was Job as he really was. Integrity doesn't exist without openness and the honest admission before God that we desperately need His forgiveness.

WHAT JOB SAYS: NO CLOSETS, NO SKELETONS

"Why me, Lord? I don't deserve all this." Every new day on the ash pile tightens Job's anguished soul another turn in the vice of suffering. In verses 33 and 34 he revisits the one issue that his friends have thrown in his face constantly: his own sin. Is he guilty of pretending to be what he's not, or is he sincere in his disclaimers about hidden sin? In this section of the oath he denies that he has concealed any misdeeds then rejects a logical rationale for why he might have played this game of camouflage.

A COVER-UP?

His first goal is to dismiss any notion that he is hiding any deep, dark scandalous crime. Even though he abridges the full "if . . . then" formula of self-judgment, Job's point is forceful: "I have (not) concealed my transgressions as others do." The verb "concealed" is literally "to cover." Job uses it with the idea of hiding evil. He was not two-faced, claiming to be one thing in public while he was something else in those off-limits corners of life no one else saw. In particular Job denies that he has glossed over "transgressions," serious acts of rebellion that would have cast doubt on his submission to God. While it's true that all of us keep some secrets—"others do," as Job says—his integrity allows him to avow that he has done his best to come clean when he has sinned.

The second line in verse 33 illustrates the point Job is making. Men in the ancient Near East could conceal items under the layered folds of their tunics. That's probably what he means by hiding something "in the bosom." Except, of course, what he's concerned with is not a literal purse or weapon tucked into a fold, but "iniquity"—secret sin that he needs to confess openly. As Herbert writes, ". . . (W)ithin my heart I made closets; and in them many a chest; And like a master in my trade, in those chests, boxes; in each box, a till . . . ." Since Job's world had a more heightened sense of shame than does ours, who could blame him for trying to save face by covering up any potential embarrassment in his portfolio?

JOB'S CATCH-22

Verse 34 brings into focus such a scenario. Peer pressure might have compelled a lesser man to bite his tongue and pretend that everything was on the up in his life. The "great fear of the multitude" he mentions is a powerful image-shaper. The word translated "fear" is an intense term rendered as "be terrified" in some places. Job's hypocrisy might also turn his own family against him, he reasons. He would become a laughingstock in his community and bring reproach on both himself and his loved ones had his secret sins surfaced. So the only thing to do was to stonewall—keep quiet and not even leave the house. That's what life as a hypocrite would have been like for Job if he had kept his sin under wraps.

As we know, however, Job's noble character kept him from living a lie. Throughout this siege of adversity he has agonized over the question of his sin. On one hand Job has never claimed that he was perfect. He prays that God would forgive his sin, if that's the problem. No one is "right" before God; we can't even clean up our own act, so to speak, because we head right back to the filth. Job knows that's the case. What he can't pinpoint, though, is any great offense he has committed which might have prompted these devastating attacks by God. He is "in the right" as best he can tell, no matter what his friends may say.

This Catch-22 dilemma poses yet another terrible irony for the scorned sufferer languishing amid the ashes. In the scenario Job presents in these two verses he fears that others would deride him should he reveal his secret sin. The reality, of course, is that they are *now* heaping ridicule and contempt upon him because they think he's hiding evil and will not confess it. Lost in all of this anguish is Job's rock solid integrity as he takes his case to the Almighty Judge. "It is the high commitment to personal integrity that motivates Job to swear this oath of innocence . . . hopefully to win a public vindication from God."

WHAT WE FACE: HIDING THE TRUTH ABOUT SECRETS

Our 21st century world is about as far from the Puritan society of New England in the 1600s as can be. Yet *The Scarlet Letter*, Nathaniel Hawthorne's morality tale of sin, guilt, and confession, is timeless in what it reveals about human personality. Reverend Dimmesdale, Hester Prynne's secret lover, hypocritically speaks of men who "go about among their fellow-creatures looking as pure as the new-fallen snow; while their hearts are all speckled and spotted with iniquity of which they cannot rid themselves." The pastor withers under the suspicions of Roger Chillingworth, but finally escapes the old man's accusing gaze when he confesses the truth of his offense on the public scaffold at high noon.

Their perceptions of hypocrisy and confession were much more lucid than ours. We often send mixed signals about secrecy. While once our culture cloistered hidden sins, today the opposite is sometimes true: telling our secrets regardless of when, how, and to whom, constitutes moral high ground. We're caught in the middle of the culture of cover-up versus the era of the exposé. We bounce back and forth from the stonewalling act of Richard Nixon to the off-the-wall acts on Jerry Springer, from buried corruption in the Roman Catholic priesthood to the bizarre "coming out" of sexual deviance on parade. At the core of *The DaVinci Code* phenomenon were charges of a centuries-old church cover-up involving the supposed "true" life of Jesus and the control of ecclesiastical authority. In these extremes or in the day-to-day secret sins of suburbia, however, we seldom run across the healing of God-driven confession.

SECRET AGENTS

At one end of the secrecy spectrum is the very thing Job denies—living falsely. Psychologist Anita Kelly is convinced that keeping secrets is more common than telling lies. "Secrets are a part of virtually every adult's life," she says, based on her empirical research. By "secrets" she's not talking about private details of life that have no place in public view, such as specific hygiene habits. She refers instead to deliberately deceiving others about who we are and what we do. Some people pretend in order to avoid embarrassment or shame, while others fear rejection and damage in close relationships. We hide things, too, in order to protect our image or reputation. Secrecy often coincides with coping strategies such as denial, when we refuse to face the truth either consciously or subconsciously.

Such a disorder also prevents a healthy relationship with God. What's more, keeping deep secrets harms our mental, physical, and family lives. Self-worth depreciates, stress builds, and the energy we have to expend covering up the lies takes a heavy toll on us psychologically. Studies also show that people who hide things from others as a way of life are more likely to be physically sick than those whose lives are open. Deception devastates families as well by dividing loyalties, creating suspicion, and clouding communication.

From a different angle, one might conclude that never before in our history have we been so open with each other. After all, one of the first principles of modern psychoanalysis is a patient's openness with the counselor. Consider, too, the popularity of encounter and recovery groups where participants share their thoughts and experiences. Everything's "on the table" and everyone is expected to come clean. On a popular level, lurid "tell-all" books and media events do just that, or so they claim. After all, "inquiring minds want to know." As Budziszewski correctly recognizes, however, " . . . (T)he tell-all never tells all; such confessions are always more or less dishonest. We may admit every detail of what we have done, *except that it was wrong.*"

"HIDE ME, O MY SAVIOR HIDE"

We may live in a culture obsessed with knowing and telling secrets, but we do not live in a culture of confession. Two things are missing. One is repentance. Confessing sin truly, according to the Bible, never occurs apart from sincere repentance. I cannot sing, "Plenteous grace with Thee is found, Grace to cover all my sin" until I have sung, "I am all unrighteousness. False and full of sin I am . . ." Unrepentant confession is usually nothing more than trying to appease the conscience, to rationalize what we've done, or to make the best of a bad situation.

The second element of confession we lack today is a God-consciousness that pervades all of life. Confession's fruit may fall in the fields of psychology and sociology, but it is rooted firmly on theology's ground. We hide secrets from others because we think God isn't watching. The church, too, is caught up in an image-crazy, accept-all and rebuke-no-one mentality to the point that we hardly ever sharpen one another's spirit through confession, rebuke, and forgiveness. When we recover the real character of a holy God who not only loves people but also sees, evaluates, and holds them accountable for everything they do, then we'll know confession as Job knew it.

WHAT WE MUST DO: "RELEASE THE POWER THAT HEALS"

I understand why I avoid confessing my sins to other people, but I'm not sure why I have trouble telling God about them. I know by now that honesty with Him is the only path to forgiveness, and waves of joy through His abundant mercy always accompany that forgiveness. My guess is that you have that problem, too. Maybe if we take the plunge today and begin the hard work of confession now, it wouldn't seem so out of character for us tomorrow, and the next day, and the next.

1. DETERMINE TO AVOID SIN IN THE FIRST PLACE. While we kid ourselves if we claim to be sinless, that fact doesn't excuse us from just giving in to sin without a fight. If you love the Lord, hate evil, commands the psalmist. That means I must stop catering to my weakness with the excuse that there's nothing I can do except commit sin. I am forever indebted to my youth pastor who continually challenged me as a teen, "Stop making provision for your flesh to do whatever it wants."

2. ADMIT THE DAMAGE UNCONFESSED SIN WILL CAUSE IN YOUR LIFE. As we have seen, untreated guilt poisons our minds, our bodies, our emotions, and our spirits. It is a systemic malignancy. David knew only too well the ravages of hidden sin, so he prayed, "Declare me innocent of hidden faults." God knows them anyway, so the sooner we own up to them and ask for His forgiveness the better. "Nothing between my soul and the Savior," the great preacher C. A. Tindley wrote, "nothing preventing the least of His favor: Keep the way clear! Let nothing between."

3. DON'T JUST TALK ABOUT CONFESSING, DO IT! As you confess, ask God to forgive you—then trust that He does. After all, forgiveness comes through Christ's work, not our sincerity, good intentions, or emotional sorrow. Our Father is full of mercy, so when we admit our guilt we can move quickly and confidently from a fear of judgment to calm assurance that He removes our transgressions "as far as the east is from the west." In seventh grade gym class, Coach Echols had all of us students line up while he demanded that the guilty person confess to shredding the tumbling mats with a knife. Coach was a gruff, burly sort of man and so intimidating in his tirade against us that most of us who had nothing to do with the crime were ready to 'fess up to it! Yet our God invites us to His dispensary of grace where we come not because He bullies us, but because He welcomes us as His children.

4. USE OPPORTUNITIES TO CONFESS SIN PUBLICLY. By all means we must use decorum and propriety in public confession, but open accountability contributes to the health of Christ's body. The setting in which we confess may be public worship, with a small group, or just to a mentor or discipleship partner. You may need to come clean with someone you have wronged or who has wronged you, as Jesus directed. I was the evangelist one evening in a revival service in Georgia when true revival descended from heaven—and I didn't say a word! The "sermon" was the people's confession to each other. As the service began, one brother approached another and wept as he confessed how he had wronged him. This one act of brazen humility started a chain of similar encounters, and before long almost everyone in the place was kneeling with someone else in brokenness and repentance. Your open confession may ignite the fires of forgiveness in your friend's life.

5. ONCE YOU HAVE CONFESSED SIN, ABANDON IT COMPLETELY. You likely won't conquer its tyranny over you in one day or overnight, but try. Besetting sins especially may involve a prolonged struggle; but lay siege to them at once and cut off the supply lines that feed them. In the heart of every Christian is a persistent longing for Christ to set us free from all sin. We begin our walk toward that goal by being honest with God. As Richard Foster puts it, "Honesty leads to confession, and confession leads to change."

6. CULTIVATE A DEEP AWARENESS OF SIN, AND LET IT BE AN ALARM IN YOUR SOUL. The only way to do this is to develop and maintain a disciplined study of God as He reveals Himself in Scripture. If you fall in love with God as He truly is, then anything which displeases Him will be an affront to you as well. You will chase anything from your heart that might threaten your relationship with the holy God who is your very life. If our knowledge of God is skimpy, our love for Him will be shallow and selfish pride will shape our thinking. We'll be at home in our culture rationalizing sin rather than at home in Christ overcoming sin.

7. CONFESS SPECIFIC SINS AT LEAST DAILY, AND MORE OFTEN AS NECESSARY. We must tell God the moment we recognize sin; and our confession should not be a "one call covers all" general statement, but a detailed, itemized one. Sometimes a false humility actually born of pride prevents us from being honest with God and with others. We're afraid of what people might think of us, or that confessing might sound "super-spiritual" and seem to indict others for their silence. As a fellowship of forgiven sinners, though, we need to hear how God helps people overcome their sins. Healing power flows when we open ourselves to let go of the past.

8. HEAR THE CONFESSION OF ANOTHER WITH MEEKNESS AND LOVE. We must apply the Golden Rule as we listen to others acknowledge their sin. How would you want them to respond to *your* confession? Recognize that all of us sin, that all of us "live under the cross" and should receive a fellow believer's admission of guilt with a heart to restore, love, and forgive. The only place in the world sin is effectively dealt with is in a relationship with God through Christ as we become members of his body, the church. Words of response probably aren't necessary as we hear confession. Just listen, pray, and weep together.

Eugene Peterson is right: "A refusal to deal with sin is a refusal to deal with relationships. And if we don't deal with relationships, we can't love." The one who conceals his sins will not prosper, says the wise man. Instead, the one who confesses and abandons them will find mercy.

CHAPTER 11

The Stewardship Promise:

Job Resolves to Be Considerate of the Land

Job 31:38–40

If my land has cried out against me
and its furrows have wept together,
if I have eaten its yield without payment
and made its owners breathe their last,
let thorns grow instead of wheat,
and foul weeds instead of barley.

The words of Job are ended.

On a typical 10-degree, snowy October afternoon in Siberia, Mike Corley and I shuddered—not so much for the cold, since we had dressed for that. No, we trembled when we realized that unspeakable horror had happened on the very ground where we stood. In a grove of white birches just outside Chelyabinsk, Russia, Josef Stalin's henchmen had fired bullets into the brains of thousands of Jewish and Orthodox Christian people. The executioners had then entombed their corpses in the shafts of the gold mines under the ground beneath our feet. Several makeshift stars of David and crosses dotted the scene, many with pictures and personal effects of the victims. A layman in the church later asked me, "And did you not hear the echo of the land weeping in agony?"

In verses 38-40, Job hears his land crying out against him. He knows that would be the effect were he guilty of abusing its workers. This unit again touches base with the way Job had treated others, in this case those who had managed his property. He declares that he had not taken advantage of them, denying even such cruelty that might have ended some of their lives prematurely. Had he been guilty, the suffering of the land itself would have exposed his sin. Job's powerful oath points to the often overlooked link between the created order and human spirituality, both subject to the rule of God.

WHAT JOB SAYS: THE LAND LAMENTS

The final statement in Job's vow of integrity involves his stewardship of the resources God had given him. He certifies that he has abused neither the land nor those who worked the land in his service. Although the three preceding verses formally "seal" the entire oath, verses 38-40 form a fitting conclusion to the vows since they deal with the physical venue in which all of Job's actions have occurred: his home territory. In another instance of the full "if/then" oath formula, this man of integrity asserts his innocence in the strongest possible terms. The first two verses lay out the condition Job assumes in his denial by means of two parallel "if" clauses, while the last verse pronounces the judgment which would follow were he guilty.

Had Job renounced his integrity by committing certain crimes, the land would "cry out" its accusations against him. Verse 38 personifies Job's home turf as a brutalized victim pointing the finger at the one responsible for its suffering. The word order in the Hebrew of the first line emphasizes that Job, the land's owner, serves as the target of this rebuke: "If *against me* my land cries out" (emphasis mine). The ground itself, the arable soil Job tills for his crops, thus becomes his accuser. The very scene of the crime serves as a witness to the misdeeds of its owner.

The parallel line in verse 38 intensifies the thought. The general subject "land" becomes the more specific "furrows." Not only does the land "cry out," but now even these cultivated rows "weep together" over Job's sins. To borrow the title of Alan Paton's great novel lamenting past injustices in South Africa, "the beloved country"—in this case Job's own property—does indeed "cry" over the moral failings of its owner.

POLLUTED LIFE, POLLUTED LAND

In the following verse, Job mentions those hypothetical sins which would have prompted such a censure from the land. Keep in mind that Job's point here, as in all of the specific oaths, is to avow his innocence of any such misconduct. The first line in verse 39 levels the charge of eating the "yield" or produce of the land "without payment." While this may describe acquiring property by illegal seizure or theft, as with Ahab's conscription of Naboth's vineyard, it more likely denotes the owner's failure to pay his workers a fair wage or in a timely manner, if he pays them at all.

Job also denies that he has "made its owners breathe their last." Since the land is Job's, these "owners" are likely the managers or stewards who oversee the property for him. The phrase, "made [them] breathe their last" carries some difficulties. However, the scene depicted here seems to be that of an owner who pushes his workers so hard with an unreasonable production quota that he hastens their deaths. What is clear is that this landowner so exploits those who work for him that even the land protests.

This notion that a person's moral and ethical conduct can have repercussions for the land itself surfaces throughout the Old Testament. Cain's murder of Abel prompted the latter's blood to cry out to God from the ground, which was cursed thereafter for Cain. Covenant violation against the Lord brought defilement to the land for the nation of Israel as well. Their degenerate worship of Canaanite idols polluted the very land itself. God's gift of the land was so essential to their covenant life and sustenance that when his people betrayed this relationship even the land suffered the effects of the covenant curse. Although the Mosaic Law code spelled out this principle specifically for Israel, Job's testimony demonstrates that it was in effect for the one who worshiped the Lord even before Moses and outside Canaan. After all Job refers here to land in Uz, not Israel. Yet because he is a devotee of the true God, all of Job's experiences, including the productivity of the land in earning his livelihood, reflect his commitment to Yahweh.

If Job had been guilty of such offenses, then "thorns" and "stinkweed" would have grown in his fields instead of "wheat" and "barley," according to verse 40. These obnoxious weeds indicate unproductive soil, ground under God's curse. What appropriate justice this would have been: since the wrong involved those who tended the soil, the soil itself now punishes the one responsible. Wheat and barley were the most lucrative grains harvested in the ancient Near East. Job's fields would produce only smelly briars, and as they sprang up so, too, would his poverty.

WHAT WE FACE: A SACRED EPIC STARRING NATURE AS "GOD"

In the spring of 2005 the desert literally blossomed like a rose. Wildflowers tinted the floor of Death Valley in California for the first time in years. Why the sudden color burst of plant life? More than six inches of rain since the previous September in an area that usually gets only two inches per year did the trick. Many ecologists traced the phenomenon to climate shifts brought on by global warming. We confront similar yet more ominous environmental issues regularly in the news: deforestation, pollution, fuel resources, overpopulation, waste management, habitat conservation—on and on goes the list.

As Christians, we typically yawn in response with a "so what" disclaimer. Here go the "greenies" and the "tree-huggers" again with their "save the spotted owl" agendas that seem far-removed from the more urgent demands of genuine spiritual living. We can't get off that easy, though, for two reasons. The first one comes from God Himself, as we'll see more closely in the next section. Job's words here confront us with God, the land, and human responsibility. As he suggests, God the Creator is intimately linked to the earth and to the people He made to inhabit it. Then, second, there's our culture. Most scientific and political concern about the environment builds on a foundation of naturalism, a view of reality that squares off directly against biblical Christianity. This worldview believes that only natural forces shape our existence. The supposed spiritual, metaphysical, and "miraculous" actually reflect nature at work, the naturalist believes.

HOW THINGS ARE

For many in the ecological wing of science, this commitment to nature becomes their religion, with the planet's ecosystem their deity, its preservation their calling, and its evolution their dogma. Listen to Ursula Goodenough in her work, tellingly titled, *The Sacred Depths of Nature*:

> Any global tradition needs to begin with a shared worldview—a culture-independent, globally accepted consensus as to how things are. From my perspective, this part is easy. How things are is, well, *how things are*: our scientific account of Nature, an account that can be called *The Epic of Evolution.*

Notice her not-so-subtle claim that this "religion" is "culture-independent"—that is, scientific and objective—and a "globally accepted consensus." Everybody believes it. It's a no-brainer; it's so easy to see. One must really be a total ignoramus not to know this, in other words.

To her, this is "religious naturalism." She calls it "religious" because it moves her to "awe and wonder at the grandeur, the poetry, the richness of natural beauty." Nature is the "cosmic Mystery" of the divine. No "creator" exists, yet she makes "a profession of

Faith" to evolutionary naturalism. Goodenough even borrows Christian hymnody in her veneration: "Immortal, Invisible, God Only Wise" and "Spirit of the Living God." The "god" of whom she sings, however, is the "elegant process" of evolution, not the God whom these hymn writers worshiped, the personal Creator God revealed through nature and in Scripture.

THE (BAD) LUCK OF THE DICE

This belief system also clashes with what a Christian worldview teaches about humans and their moral responsibility. To the naturalist, humans are simply another part of the "biophilia," or living world, on the same level and of no greater importance than any other species. In fact, Edward Wilson speaks for many scientists when he labels people "an environmental hazard." He contends, "Darwin's dice have rolled badly for the earth. It was a misfortune for the living world in particular . . . that a carnivorous primate [humans] and not some more benign form of animal made the breakthrough [to intelligent, rational control of the earth]." You see, we are "tribal and aggressively territorial," "selfish," and uncooperative with our environment. We eat too much meat, use the sun at too low of an efficiency level, pollute the air, and . . . well, you get the picture.

According to naturalists, why should we think that humans harbor any sense of "responsibility" at all? The only "moral reasoning" or "rules" we possess have "evolved genetically because they confer survival and reproduction on human beings," Wilson claims. Might makes right, that is. Justice, equity, sacrifice, compassion—the very issues Job wrestles with—do not fit well into a worldview energized by natural selection.

AN OFF-LIMITS GOD

In standard 21st century ecological thought, we are therefore left with an explanation of God, humans, and the world that allows for no reality beyond nature's borders. Goodenough perceives and, sadly, laments her dilemma:

> So we arrive here at what is, for many, the heart of it all. If there is a major tension between an approach like religious naturalism and the monotheistic religions [including Christianity], it centers on the question of whether or not one believes in a personal god . . . For me, and probably for all of us, the concept of a personal, interested god can be appealing, often deeply so. In times of sorrow or despair, I often wonder what it would be like to pray to God . . . and believe that I was heard, believe that my petition might be answered . . . But in the end, such faith is simply not available to me. I can't do it. I lack the resources to render my capacity for love and to be loved to Supernatural Beings. And so I have no choice but to pour these capacities and needs into earthly relationships, fragile and mortal and difficult as they are.

Of course, she does have a choice. All of us do. God's "invisible attributes, namely his eternal power and divine nature, have been clearly perceived, ever since the creation of the world . . . (S)o they are without excuse."

WHAT WE MUST DO: LIVE AS WISE "EARTHKEEPERS"

Psalm 104 is one of my favorite poems in the Psalter. A hymn of thanksgiving, it inventories God's works in creation, from His messenger winds to the nesting birds in the cedars of Lebanon. The main premise appears in the middle of the psalm, as is true with many Hebrew poems: "O LORD, how manifold are your works! In wisdom have you made them all; the earth is full of your creatures." Our responsibility to act as "earthkeepers" begins here.

1. WE MUST SEE ALL OF LIFE THROUGH THE LENS OF A GOD-CENTERED WORLDVIEW. Our actions toward all of God's creation must flow from His revealed truth in Scripture about why He made both the earth and those of us who live on it. The "landscape plotted and pieced—fold, fallow, and plow; and all the trades, their gear and tackle and trim" are those "dappled things," G. M. Hopkins reminds us, that bring God glory.

2. BELIEVERS SHOULD CARRY OUT THEIR STEWARDSHIP MISSION INTENTIONALLY TO HONOR CHRIST. The cultural mandate of Genesis one requires wisdom. How do I balance my responsibility to "subdue" earth's produce in a way that will meet human need and yet ensure that my descendants will have the chance to do the same? That is, how do we both develop and conserve the planet's resources? As we live frugally and simply, we express a land ethic not derived from a "green power" bumper sticker mindset where nature is god, but from a biblical land ethic giving honor to a wise Creator. Yet the breadth of this stewardship extends to how we live *in* our environment as well: the effort we give to our work, the way we raise our children, what entertains us and makes us laugh, how we spend our money, what we do with the gospel, the way we treat the disabled—add more to the list to fit your life.

3. USE CREATION TO MEET PEOPLE'S NEEDS. God calls us to help those we can help with our time, our labor, our money, and our love. We dare not look the other way and close our hearts when we have resources that relieve human suffering; when we do, we actually testify of how little the gospel has impacted our own lives. People reflect the image of God no matter who they are, and He calls us not to shun or exploit them but to care for them with what He places in our hand. Find someone near you who needs your help and give it.

4. PART OF LIVING IN CHRIST IS ANTICIPATING HIS NEW CREATION. He promises a "new earth" free from the corrupting blemishes our rebellion has brought to this one. Until fulfillment of the kingdom arrives, we express our loyalty to Him now by "putting off" those sins tied to our lives before we were in Christ and "putting on" moral behavior reflecting His holiness. We need the reminder that land suffers when people sin.

5. DON'T MISS THE WONDER OF GOD'S CREATION. Buck the trend of our jaded, "nothing-phases-me" culture and cultivate a sense of awe toward the unmatched beauty of God's handiwork. The skyline of those gleaming "alabaster cities" may be impressive, but God's "purple mountain majesty" dwarfs all of them! Let yourself sigh at the copper glow of a coastal sunset. Drink in the sensory overload of a steady summer shower in the forested mountains. Then bow your knee and still your heart in humble gratitude and submission to the God who designed all these splendors and who planned to let you enjoy them today. And know that He has so much more to let you in on.

CONCLUSION

Thorny Crown, Integrity's Crown

Job 31:35-37

Oh, that I had one to hear me!
(Here is my signature! Let the Almighty answer me!)
Oh, that I had the indictment written by my adversary!
Surely I would carry it on my shoulder;
I would bind it on me as a crown;
I would give him an account of all my steps;
like a prince I would approach him.

Everything Job has said in the book until now comes to a head in this exclamation. He can't contain himself before finishing his oath. Instead this bold, impassioned cry bursts into the context. The matter cannot continue unresolved for Job. It's as if this innocent martyr lays bare his heart and rolls his raw emotions over it to plead, "I can't go on without an answer! You see and know my life, O God—let me know where I stand! Tell me what's happening!" This is not impudent bravado, but a heart begging to bask in the favor of God's smile. Great relief and deep anguish meet in Job's full-throated appeal for the Almighty's answer.

Three refrains echo through his cry. First is his intense longing for God. Though Job walked with God in an intimate, trusting relationship, he is alone now, desperate and away from home, restless in his misery. Throughout the book Job has sought a hearing with *Shaddai*, only to find instead an echo of emptiness as he awaited an answer. Little does he realize how the silence of God will soon end in a whirlwind encounter! Anyone who knows God must prepare for a season in his relationship when God seems distant and His voice stilled. Here's where our trust is tested the most; yet here, too, is where it often grows the most.

Our longing for God in those times is radically different from the soul without Him, the sufferer on the outside looking in to the possibility of faith. For that person I must correct what threatens to be a fatal misconception. Job has touted his innocence at great length in this disclaimer. Like a skilled museum docent, he has interpreted an exhibit of integrity piece-by-piece—not as a disinterested guide, but as a fervent advocate. Do not think, however, that a person can begin a relationship with God simply by pursuing integrity through a blameless lifestyle. Please dismiss such a notion altogether from your thinking. The only way to meet God is through trust, a total dependence on Him as you take His word for what He provides. Integrity is the *result of* knowing God, not the *means to* know Him. It expresses our life in God.

The second refrain in Job's plea concerns the very problem that keeps us from knowing God and practicing integrity: the question of innocence. Job argues convincingly that he is not guilty of the charges detailed in his oath. In verse 35 he demands to see the indictment listing his crimes. He has "signed" his petition authenticating it as a legal document. He knows that were his accuser to file the warrant, it would be totally blank. He has committed none of these wrongs.

As we know, however, Job *is* a sinner. He may not face conviction for these particular charges, but even this good man, this man of integrity, stands condemned before the holy God. So do all of us. Our rap sheet is not blank. The charges against us are too many to count. Every violation of God's holy character, whether we are aware of the offense or not, finds its way to our slate of offenses. As a result any possibility of integrity, any chance that we might live the life Job describes here seems hopeless.

Job seems to find a glimmer of hope, though. He expects vindication. When it comes, his relief will be so exhilarating that he'll parade it in the streets and through the town gate. Job will "wear" that canceled indictment like a splendid new robe so that everyone will see it. God's favor will be his crown! With all the confidence of a prince, he will approach the throne as a royal child, the son of the King.

How can Job be so confident? What gives him his hope? The third refrain gives us the answer. He has hinted at it all along, here and there all the way through the book. He speaks of an "arbiter" who will touch both him and *Shaddai* to bring reconciliation. "I have one who testifies for me on high," Job declares, "who will be my advocate before God." This Redeemer will one day stand on earth in Job's defense. His mediator will show Job mercy, deliver him by means of a ransom, and restore his joy in fellowship with God.

Job's advocate is the one to whom we must also turn. Jesus wore a crown of thorns so that we might wear integrity's crown. On His cross He canceled "the record of debt that stood against us with its legal demands." He set it aside, "nailing it to the cross." Those of us who claim Jesus as our advocate have a blank indictment, too—not because of our integrity, but because of Jesus' perfect record and His willingness to pay our fine for our guilt.

In that hour of darkness, outcast on Golgotha's ash heap, the solitary figure on the cross wearing the thorny crown bore all humanity's hopes for innocence. When the trial and execution were over, amid the ruins of sin and death and guilt, the victor's crown had replaced the thorns. When we embrace the Man and His cross with total trust, we may then approach the throne as children of the King. The work of Christ in our hearts opens the door to the will of God in our lives. Integrity may crown our lives after all because Christ is being formed in us. Kingdom life is a life of integrity, a whole life lived inside-out.

So what is inward turns outward
as does, we are told, the Kingdom of God.
So we contain that which contains us.

A PRAYER FOR INTEGRITY BASED ON JOB 31

Lord *Shaddai*, Almighty One,

I gladly confess that wholeness is perfected only in You. You dwell in light that I cannot approach in the gloom of my own guilt. Yet I know my Redeemer lives to empower me with His Spirit for a life of integrity. In the ashes of my shame, I yearn only for Your glory as my crown.

Teach me to love holy thinking. Tear away from my mind corrupt images that leave my life spotted with lust's dark stains.

Shame me today when I resort to telling a lie. In the moments following, show me the bloody body of the One nailed to the cross for nothing but truth.

Deliver my will from its slavery to money's clutches. Turn my heart to find all I need in the generous supply flowing from Your heart of grace.

Help me to keep every promise I make, but to promise only what honors You. Each moment of today renew my commitment not to betray the trust of those who are counting on me.

Satisfy my thirst for what is true and right by saturating my life with loyalty to Your covenant. Open my eyes to see every person I meet today as Your image-bearer so that I may treat them as You would.

Fashion my heart to give as Yours does, O Lord. Grant that someone's life will be better at the end of the day because You have loved that one through me.

Be to me this day and every day all that I love, all that I need, all that I seek, and all that I am. Make my heart bold to drive away quickly any affection unworthy of You.

Remind me of what it was like to try to live without Your forgiveness. Grace all of my relationships with Your mind of mercy.

Rebuke my vain attempts to hide from You, Father. Bring me to the place where no secrets ever cast a shadow between us.

Govern my hands through a mind which You alone control, so that everything they give will truly come from You.

Receive glory in everything I do today, my King. With all my heart, mind, and will, I ask You to rule over my life without rival.

Through Him who is my ransom, my daysman, my crown—Jesus. Amen.

INDEX

Persons

A

B

C

D

E

F

G

H

J

K

L

M

N

O

P

R

S

T

W

Y

Z

INDEX

Scripture References

JUDGES

1 SAMUEL

2 SAMUEL

1 KINGS

JOB

PSALMS

NOTES

PREFACE

vii *"Doctrine and life . . . and awe."* George Herbert, "The Windows" in *George Herbert: The Complete English Poems*, ed. John Tobin (London: Penguin, 1991), 61.

vii *"You know, the one ... uh, Christianity."* Accessed at www.thesimpsonsquotes.com.

viii *Despite the fervor . . . claims Jeffrey L. Sheler.* Jeffrey L. Sheler, "Nearer My God to Thee," *U. S. News and World Report*, 3 May 2004, 59-60.

viii *Instead of Christian . . . Alan Wolfe contends.* Cited in Sheler, 66.

ix-x *"The final component . . . psychologist Judy TenElshof.* Judy TenElshof, "Encouraging the Character Formation of Future Christian Leaders," *Journal of the Evangelical Theological Society* 42 (1999): 81.

CHAPTER 1: A PROMISE KEPT

1 *"The book [of Job] . . . Yancey reminds us.* Philip Yancey, *The Bible Jesus Read* (Grand Rapids: Zondervan, 1999), 52.

1 *Three times . . . away from evil."* The references are 1:1, 8 and 2:3. See also Job's claims in 9:21 and 12:4.

1 *"If I wash . . . abhor me."* Job 9:30–31. Job also confronts the reality of his own sinfulness in Job 7:20–21; 9:28; 10:6; 13:26; and 14:16–17.

1-2 *Following the enormous . . . blessed God's name."* Job 1:20–22.

2 *Even Eliphaz . . . as much.* Job 4:3–4.

2 *The leading officials . . . bereft townspeople.* See the honor afforded Job in chapter 29.

2 *The Lord . . . his integrity."* Job 2:3.

2 *Job's wife . . . speaks of it.* Job 2:9.

2 *He himself . . . from me."* Job's statements of faith are impressive in 13:15; 14:14; 16:19–21; 19:25–27; 23:8–12; and 27:4–6.

2-3 *As Francis Andersen . . . taken as genuine."* Francis I. Andersen, *Job: An Introduction and Commentary* (Downers Grove: InterVarsity, 1976), 66.

4 *People loved . . . his troops."* Job 29:25.

4 *"But now . . . laugh at me."* Job 30:1.

4 *Job languishes . . . endless pain.* Job 30:29.

4 *His prosperity . . . from a tree.* Job 30:15, 30.

4 *The reason for . . . you persecute me."* Job 30:19–21.

4 *Those who heard . . . in the ancient world.* On the legal background of Job 31, see Michael Brennan Dick, "The Legal Metaphor in Job 31," *Catholic Biblical Quarterly* 41 (1979): 37-50.

5 *Earlier in the book . . . his innocence.* See Job 23:10–12 and 27:2–6.

5 *Job publicly announces . . . specific punishment.* The full "if . . . then" oath formula occurs in verses 7–8; 9–10; 16, 19, 20, 21, 22; and 38, 39, 40. A partial form is in 5-6; 13; 24, 25, 26; 29, 31; and 33.

5 *Similar statements . . . in the Old Testament.* See Psalm 7:4–5 and 137:5–6. For brief declarations of innocence not using this format, see Numbers 16:15 and 1 Samuel 24:10–16.

7 *Lewis Smedes . . . they make"* Lewis B. Smedes, "The Power of Promises," in *A Chorus of Witnesses*, eds. Thomas G. Long and Cornelius Plantinga, Jr. (Grand Rapids: Eerdmans, 1994), 156.

7-8 *God, who made . . . his good pleasure."* Philippians 2:13.

8 *What's more . . . Christ was born.* In considering the date of Job, two separate questions are at issue. One involves when the book was written and the other deals with the historical setting in which Job lived. As to the latter, most clues in the book itself point to patriarchal times, around 2000 B. C., as the time for the events of the book: the family organization and decentralized worship, the name *Shaddai* (used 31 times in Job), Job's lifespan of 140 years after his restoration, and the use of the Hebrew word *kĕśîṭâ* for "piece of money" in 42:11. The book could have been written then or, as is more likely, in the wisdom age of Solomon around the first millennium B. C. See the discussion in Raymond B. Dillard and Tremper Longman III, *An Introduction to the Old Testament* (Grand Rapids: Zondervan, 1994), 200-1.

8 *Uz, his homeland . . . Arabia border.* See G. Frederick Owen, "The Land of Uz" in *Sitting with Job: Selected Studies on the Book of Job*, ed. Roy B. Zuck (Grand Rapids: Baker, 1992), 245-47.

CHAPTER 2: THE PURITY PROMISE

11 *In fact, Simon . . . curmudgeons.* Simon Blackburn, *Lust* (New York: Oxford University Press, 2004), 3.

13 *The word translated ... elsewhere in the book.* See Job 11:11, 23:15, 32:12, 37:14, and 38:18.

13 *"Then desire ... James affirms.* James 1:15

13 *Assuming his guilt . . . do not know God."* Job 18:22.

13 *In his first speech . . . reap the same."* Job 4:8.

14 *Jesus reminds us . . . sexual immorality. . . ."* Mark 7:21.

14 *The fact that . . . ultimate vindication.* Job 23:10.

14 *He anticipates . . . altogether."* Psalm 139:2–4.

15 *The pop artist . . . up and down." Dangerously in Love*, Beyonce Knowles, Sony CD B000099T2L, 2003.

15 *This becomes . . . and dialogue."* Rebecca Hagelin, "MTV's Poisoning a Generation," Crosswalk.com, at www.crosswalk.com/news/1319399.html?view=point.

15 *A study by . . . online.* Shawn Hubler, "Porn Part of Culture for Today's Teenagers," *The* (Nashville) *Tennessean*, 24 April 2005, 23A.

15 *What does it say . . . one woman?* Terrance Dean, "Metro Says It Can't Prosecute Creators of Pornographic Movie," *The* (Nashville) *Tennessean*, 11 April 2005, 4B.

16 *A disciple's walk . . . way we think.* Romans 12:1–2.

16 *Our goal . . . obey Christ."* 2 Corinthians 10:5.

16 *John Piper . . . image or thought.* John Piper, *Pierced by the Word* (Sisters, OR: Multnomah, 2003), 69-73.

17 *God lives within . . . of His body.* 1 Corinthians 6:9, 12:27.

17 *His intent . . . our bodies.* 1 Corinthians 6:18–19.

17 *Emulate Joseph . . . against God."* Genesis 39:9.

17 *"Make no provision . . . counsels Paul.* Romans 13:14.

18 *Thank God . . . sexual impurity*. 1 Corinthians 6:11.

18 *But we dare not . . . God's holiness*. Romans 6:1.

18 *No wonder . . . shall see God."* Matthew 5:8.

CHAPTER 3: THE HONESTY PROMISE

19 *"The stories gets. . . sayin goes."* Cormac McCarthy, *No Country for Old Men* (New York: Alfred A. Knopf, 2005), 123.

19 *Which I reckon . . . rock is gone*. McCarthy, 123.

20 *"Falsehood is . . . full of praise." Nicomachean Ethics*, trans. H. Rackham (London: William Heinemann, 1934), book 4, chapter 7.

21 *A "false" thing . . . Delitzsch explains*. F. Delitzsch, "Job" in *Commentary on the Old Testament*, vol. IV (n. d.; rpt., Grand Rapids: Eerdmans, 1975), 176.

21 *In fact, he has ... wicked person*. Job 7:3 and 15:31.

21 *It shows up . . . full of lies*. Genesis 29:25; Psalm 34:13, 36:3.

21 *A shifty merchant . . . his customer*. Leviticus 19:35–36; Proverbs 2:16, 23, 11:1.

22 *Ralph Keyes . . . post-truth era."* Ralph Keyes, *The Post-Truth Era: Dishonesty and Deception in Contemporary Life* (New York: St. Martin's Press, 2004), 5.

22 *"It's now as . . . twice about it."* Keyes, 3.

22 *Country singer Patty Loveless . . . lovin' heart."* Harlan Howard and Kostas Lazarides, "Blame It on Your Heart," by Patty Loveless, *Only What I Feel*, Epic EK53236.

23 *"Online, the whole . . . Michel Marriott*. Cited in Keyes, 200.

23 *Psychologist Robert . . . of conversation*. David Livingstone Smith, *Why We Lie: The Evolutionary Roots of Deception and the Unconscious Mind* (New York: St. Martin's, 2004), 15.

23 *Even though this . . . truth altogether*. For the designation "alt.ethics," see Keyes, 13.

23 *As Keyes observes . . . to name a few*. Keyes, 13-16.

23 *David Nyberg claims . . . overrated."* David Nyberg, *The Varnished Truth: Truth Telling and Deceiving in Ordinary Life* (Chicago: University of Chicago Press, 1993), 3.

24 *Lauren Slater faked . . . separation from God."* Lauren Slater, *Lying: A Metaphorical Memoir* (New York: Random House, 2000), 201-2.

24 *"Do not lie . . . at Colossae*. Colossians 3:9.

24 *"Lie not . . . George Herbert*. George Herbert, *The Complete English Poems*, ed. John Tobin (London: Penguin, 1991), 8.

24 *David Gill contends . . . say otherwise."* David W. Gill, *Doing Right: Practicing Ethical Principles* (Downers Grove: InterVarsity Press, 2004), 288.

25 *Keyes notes . . . my troth."* Keyes, 23.

25 *In* Crime and Punishment *. . . could drive her."* Fyodor Dostoevsky, *Crime and Punishment*, trans. Michael Scammell (New York: Washington Square Press, 1963), 214.

25-26 *So it was with Job . . . clear and straight*. Herbert, 66.

CHAPTER 4: THE CONTENTMENT PROMISE

27 *"You know ... to live comfortably."* Accessed at http://www.cbsnews.com/stories/2005/08/14/sunday/printable777041.shtml.

28 *Reinhold Niebuhr . . . from falling."* Cited in David Wells, *Above All Earthly Powers* (Grand Rapids: Eerdmans, 2005), 41.

28 *Job now asserts . . . not turned aside."* See Job 23:11 where three of the words used here occur: "step," "way," and "turn."

28-29 *As in verse four . . . Gordis calls it.* Robert Gordis, *The Book of Job* (New York: The Jewish Theological Seminary of America, 1978), 346.

29 *Earlier in the book . . . righteous deeds.* See Job 11:14, 16:17, and 22:30.

29 *"The uprooting . . . explains Hartley.* John E. Hartley, "Job" in the *New International Commentary on the Old Testament* (Grand Rapids: Eerdmans, 1988), 412.

29 *These are usually . . . worship words!* See "confidence" in Job 8:14 and Psalm 78:7; "trust" in Psalm 40:4 and 71:15; and "rejoice" in Job 22:19 and Psalm 32:11, 21.

30 *No matter how "much" . . . suggested earlier.* Job 4:6.

30 *David Wells labels . . . consumer desire."* David Wells, *Above All Earthly Powers* (Grand Rapids: Eerdmans, 2005), 38.

30 *According to one . . . machine(s)."* Cited in Steven Garber, *The Fabric of Faithfulness* (Downers Grove: InterVarsity, 1996), 79.

30 *In 1982 there were . . . exploded to 132.* Phyllis A. Tickle, *Greed* in The Seven Deadly Sins (New York: Oxford, 2004), 44.

30 *Consider the following . . . is ludicrous. . . . "* T. Harv Eker, *Secrets of the Millionaire Mind* (New York: Harper Business, 2005), 61, 71, 99, 115.

31 *Must be the money . . . Must be the money!* Deion Sanders, *Power, Money, and Sex* (Nashville: Word, 1999), 92.

32 *God designed us . . . as it comes.* The phrase "the sacred thirst for gold" is used of the New World explorers. See Peter L. Bernstein, *The Power of Gold* (New York: John Wiley and Sons, 2000), 131.

32 *Based on studies . . . of a tithe."* Ronald J. Sider, *The Scandal of the Evangelical Conscience* (Grand Rapids: Baker, 2005), 20-1.

32 *Francis Schaeffer . . . city dump.* Francis Schaeffer, *No Little People* (Downers Grove: InterVarsity, 1984), 259.

33 *"To love . . . Ellul charges.* Jacques Ellul, *Money and Power* (Downers Grove: InterVarsity, 1984), 84.

33 *Don't forget . . . kingdom of heaven."* Matthew 19:23.

33 *First century Macedonian . . . for us.* 2 Corinthians 8:3-5.

33 *Yancey's admission . . . eternal dividends."* Philip Yancey, *Rumors of Another World* (Grand Rapids: Zondervan, 2003), 211.

33 *We must resist . . . of the self."* Wells, 41.

34 *Herbert's words . . . on forty."* Herbert, 12.

34 *Giving is thus . . . and selling."* Ellul, 110.

34 *The problem comes . . . we could help.* See Ezekiel 28:4–5 and 1 John 3:17.

34 *Shakespeare's Portia . . . well satisfied."* *The Merchant of Venice*, eds. David Bevington and David Scott Kastan (New York: Bantam, 2005), 4.1.413.

34 *While they . . . an abiding one."* Hebrews 10:33–34.

CHAPTER 5: THE LOYALTY PROMISE

35 *When the reality . . . with someone else.* Accessed at www.seinolgy.com/scripts/script-37.shtml.

36 *Statistics show . . . their spouses.* See www.morc.uchicago.edu for the 21% and 11% numbers. For the 33 and 25 percentages, see Samuel and Cynthia Janus, *The Janus Report on Sexual Behavior* (New York: John Wiley and Sons, 1993), 169.

36 *And now his . . .God and die."* Job 2:9.

37 *Like the seductive . . . smooth words."* Proverbs 7:5.

37 *The verb "entice" . . . is involved.* See Exodus 22:16; Judges 14:15, 16:5; and Hosea 2:14.

37 *Ironically . . . her lover.* See Proverbs 7:12.

37 *He denies . . . veils his face."* See Job 24:15.

38 *This notion . . . in the Old Testament.* For an example, see Achan and his family in Joshua 7. See also Deuteronomy 28:30 and 2 Samuel 12:11.

38 *The Hebrew word . . . and prostitution.* See Leviticus 18:27, 19:29; Jeremiah 13:27; Ezekiel 16:27, 22:9, 11; 23:21, 27.

39 *Job sees adultery . . . chambers of death."* See Proverbs 6:27–28, 7:27.

41 *Those "little foxes" ... the vines."* Song of Solomon 2:15.

41 *If you read . . . lifestyle of worship*. See Proverbs 2:16–19 with 2:1–4, 20; 5:3–22 with 5:1–2, 23; 7:5–23 with 7:1–2; 23:27–28 with 23:26; Matthew 5:27-28 in the context of the Sermon on the Mount addressed to those living in God's kingdom; Galatians 5:19 with 5:16; Hebrews 13:4 with 12:28 and the entire hortatory thrust of Hebrews.

42 *Whatever happens . . . all things."* 1 Corinthians 13:7.

42 *As Lauren Winner . . . rhythms of marriage."* Lauren F. Winner, *Real Sex: The Naked Truth about Chastity* (Grand Rapids: Brazos, 2005), 120.

CHAPTER 6: THE EQUITY PROMISE

45 *Gil Bouton . . . forever, I hope."* Ernest J. Gaines, *A Gathering of Old Men* (New York: Vintage, 1983), 143.

46 *We long for . . . says Terry White.* Terry White, ed., *Justice Denoted: The Legal Thriller in American, British, and Continental Courtroom Literature* (Westport, CT: Praeger, 2003), xviii.

46 *The demise of . . . by biblical religion.* Rodney Stark, *The Victory of Reason* (New York: Random House, 2005), 30.

46 *Christianity's "belief . . . of equal rights."* Stark, 76.

46 *"Very many . . . we're told.* Job 1:3.

47 *The word translated . . . action or case.* Hebrew *mišpaṭ*. This term occurs over 400 times in the Old Testament, 23 in Job.

47 *Its root meaning . . . God Himself.* For "justice" as an essential trait of Yahweh, see Psalm 33:5, 97:2, 99:4; Isaiah 30:18, 61:8.

47 *Bildad, Elihu . . . in the book.* See Job 8:3, 34:12, and 9:19.

47 *The idea of . . . in the book.* For *rîb*, "lawsuit," or "argument" in Job, see 9:3, 10:2, 13:8, 19, 23:6, 33:13, and 40:2.

48 *We find . . . human nature.* Hartley, 415; Andersen, 242.

48 *Job has already . . . in the womb.* See Job 10:10-11.

49 *From Plato and . . . human action.* Plato's *Republic* is the most detailed treatise on justice in classical writings. See Ronald H. Nash, *Social Justice and the Christian Church* (Milford, MI: Mott Media, 1983), 28–31; and Charles W. Colson, *Justice That Restores* (Wheaton: Tyndale, 2001), 17–18.

49 *Wright's statements . . . genetic stratagem."* Robert Wright, *The Moral Animal* (New York: Vintage, 1994), 205.

50 *Wright concludes . . . genes through generations.* Wright, 339.

50 *Many of Singer's . . . of killing it. . . ."* Peter Singer, *Writings on an Ethical Life* (New York: HarperCollins, 2000), 186.

50 *"Either we are . . . for it to be."* Colson, 15-16.

50 *When society jettisons . . . of the moment."* J. Budziszewski here concurs with Francis Shaeffer's assessment. *Evangelicals in the Public Square* (Grand Rapids: Baker, 2006), 76.

51 *Nancy Pearcey quotes . . . which we desire.'"* Nancy Pearcey, *Total Truth* (Wheaton: Crossway, 2004), 237-8. See also Colson, 23; and Phyllis Schlafly, *The Supremacists* (Dallas: Spence, 2004), 103-112.

51 *Do you see . . . the blessing."* Steven A. McKinion, ed., *Ancient Christian Commentary on Scripture,* Old Testament X: Isaiah 1-39 (Downers Grove: InterVarsity, 2004), 17.

51-52 *Remember James' rebuke . . . with evil thoughts?* James 2:1-4.

52 *Jesus cautions . . . with right judgment.* John 7:24.

52 *Echoing Job's square . . . no partiality*. Ephesians 6:9.

53 *One of the reasons . . . well-being of the community.* Romans 13:3-4.

53 *"The just purposes . . . argues J. Budziszewski.* Budziszewski, 25.

53 *After all . . . the two worlds*. Philip Yancey, *Rumors of Another World* (Grand Rapids: Zondervan, 2003), 187.

CHAPTER 7: THE COMPASSION PROMISE

56 *"But there will . . . among you."* Deuteronomy 15:4.

56 *"For you always . . . with you."* Matthew 26:11.

56 *Compassion asks . . . being human.* Henri J. M. Nouwen, Donald P. McNeill, and Douglas A. Morrison, *Compassion: A Reflection on the Christian Life* (New York: Doubleday, 1983), 4.

56 *Earlier in the book . . . were crushed."* Job 22:7–9.

57 *Job later . . . to the needy. . . ."* Job 29:12, 13, 16.

59 *"They're hypocrites . . . do anything."* Alan Doswald, "The Largest Company in Your City," *Christianity Today*, January 2005, 50.

59 *After the two . . . in Fresno.* Doswald, 50.

60 *Bob Lupton's FCS . . . high risk families.* Marvin Olasky, "Wins and Losses," *World*, 22 October 2005, 30-1.

60 *So many of . . . caring companions.* Estimates say that 50 million are disabled in the United States and 200 million across the globe. "Fear Not the Disabled," *Christianity Today*, November 2005, 28.

60 *Said Frederick . . . civil society . . . ."* Olasky, "Charitable Consistency," *World*, 15 April 2006, 44.

60 *As Doswald notes . . . in town."* Doswald, 50.

60-61 *His church . . . is mobilization."* Doswald, 50.

61 *"I have stacked . . . he reflects.* John Weaver, *Inside Afghanistan* (Nashville: Nelson, 2002), 184.

61 *"We will continue . . . for life."* Weaver, 197.

61 *Peter's words . . . a humble mind."* 1 Peter 3:8.

61 *As Yancey says . . . can't love.* Yancey, *Finding God in Unexpected Places* (Ann Arbor: Servant, 1997), 159.

63 *Paul says that . . . came with it.* 2 Corinthians 4:1.

63 *After all, when . . . good works.* Ephesians 2:10.

63 *Jesus "went about . . . good."* Acts 10:38.

63 *As Brennan Manning . . . were in need."* Brennan Manning, *The Importance of Being Foolish* (San Francisco: HarperCollins, 2005), 119-120.

63 *"To invite people . . . Winner suggests.* Winner, *Mudhouse Sabbath* (Brewster, MA: Paraclete Press, 2003), 46-7.

64 *When Laura Belle Barnard . . . the Bread of Life.* Laura Belle Barnard, *Touching the Untouchables* (Wheaton: Tyndale, 1985), 67.

CHAPTER 8: THE WORSHIP PROMISE

67 *Based on inscriptions . . . also called.* Kenneth G. Hoglund, "Edomites," in *Peoples of the Old Testament World*, eds. Alfred J. Hoerth, Gerald L. Mattingly, and Edwin M. Yamauchi (Grand Rapids: Baker, 1994), 345-47.

67 *He may be describing . . . in heaven."* "A Midsummer Night's Dream" in *The Portable Shakespeare* (New York: Penguin, 1977), 398.

68 *It describes . . . the same way.* See Judges 14:15 and 16:5.

68 *A most relevant . . . worship them."* Deuteronomy 11:16.

68 *Had he fallen . . . openly and outwardly."* Delitzsch, 190.

68 *Pliny alludes . . . and Lucian.* See Delitzsch, 188.

68 *The Lord commends . . . "kissed" Baal.* 1 Kings 19:18.

68 *Hosea describes . . . had crafted.* Hosea 13:2.

68 *"Behold, I . . . no further."* Job 40:4-5.

69 *"A God Begotten . . . Fallen Heart.* The expression is from A. W. Tozer, *The Knowledge of the Holy* (San Francisco: Harper and Row, 1961), 11.

70 *Alan Wolfe . . . "otherworldy reverence."* Alan Wolfe, *The Transformation of American Religion* (New York: Free Press, 2003), 35.

70-71 *While his diagnosis . . . in worship.* See, for example, Daniel M. Harrell, "Post-Contemporary Worship," *Leadership*, Spring 1999, 37-39.

71 *"The idolatrous heart . . . Tozer argues.* Tozer, *Knowledge*, 11.

71 *At the same time . . . Tozer puts it.* See Tozer, *Worship: The Missing Jewel* (Camp Hill, PA: Christian Publications, 1992), 22-23.

71 *In the sacred . . . Holy One.* Habakkuk 3:4.

71 *As the psalmist . . . may be feared."* Psalm 130:4.

72 *Eugene Peterson reminds us . . . can manipulate.* Eugene Peterson, *Christ Plays in Ten Thousand Places* (Grand Rapids: Eerdmans, 2005), 177.

72 *God's larger purpose . . . of holiness . . . ."* Tozer, *Worship*, 8.

73 *Remember, "the friendship . . . fear him."* Psalm 25:14.

74 *If we can glorify . . . to belong.* See 1 Corinthians 10:31 and 6:20.

74 *"All worship . . . Herbert remarks.* Herbert, 72.

74 *In whatever . . . enjoyment."* Tozer, Worship, 19.

74 *N. T. Wright . . . worship him."* N. T. Wright, *Simply Christian* (San Francisco: HarperSanFrancisco, 2006), 143.

75 *In a Sunday . . . heart for idols.* Robert Murray McCheyne, *Memoir and Remains of Robert Murray McCheyne*, ed. Andrew A. Bonar (Edinburgh: Oliphant, Anderson, and Ferrier, 1892), 504. The text for his sermon was Hosea 14:8.

CHAPTER 9: THE FORGIVENESS PROMISE

78 *"It's in line . . . as a human being."* Laura Blumenfeld, *Revenge: A Story of Hope* (New York: Simon and Schuster, 2002), 202.

78 *Through history . . . gotten even."* Lamech's song is in Genesis 4:23-24.

78 *Bernhard Duhm puts it . . . that crown."* Cited in H. H. Rowley, *The Book of Job* in The New Century Bible Commentary, eds. Ronald E. Clements and Matthew Black (Grand Rapids: Eerdmans, 1970), 203.

79 *We can almost . . . things are."* Job 5:27 in Peterson, *The Message Remix* (Colorado Springs: Navigators, 2003).

79 *"How dare you . . . at Job.* Job 20:2 in Peterson, *The Message Remix.*

80 *God is "angry" . . . of the wicked.* Job 9:13 and 21:17.

80 *Their "heritage" . . . like a flood."* See Job 27:13-23.

80 *"Let my enemy . . . away his life?"* Job 27:7–8.

80 *"The literary . . . Peter French.* Peter A. French, *The Virtues of Vengeance* (Lawrence: The University Press of Kansas, 2001), 3.

80 *"I'm here to . . . in* Unforgiven. Cited in French, 40.

81 *In response to the . . . set it right!" Hamlet*, Folger edition, eds. Louis B. Wright and Virginia A. LaMar (New York: Washington Square Press, 1970), 4.5.215-216.

81 *He later concedes . . . for revenge." Hamlet*, Folger, 3.2.264-265.

81 *By nature . . . someone injures us."* See Martha Nussbaum, "Equality and Mercy" in *Sex and Social Justice* (Oxford: Oxford University Press, 1999), 157.

81 *Revenge, they say . . . our self-respect."* French, x-xi; 33-34.

81-82 *Loving our enemies . . . Michael Moore suggests."* Michael Moore, "The Moral Worth of Retribution" in *Responsibility, Character, and Emotions*, ed. Ferdinand Schoeman (Cambridge: The University Press), 1987), 188.

82 *Recently, however . . . interpersonal forgiveness."* The phrase "interpersonal forgiveness" occurs often in recent literature. See, for example, Robert Karen, *The Forgiving Self* (New York: Doubleday, 2001).

82 *Their parents . . . in their hearts."* Accessed at <http://www.cbsnews.com/stories/2005/07/18/earlyshow/living/main709699.shtml>.

83 *We can't control . . . in* our *experience."* Yancey, *What's So Amazing About Grace* (Grand Rapids: Zondervan, 1997), 96.

83 *"Forgive one another . . . forgave you."* Ephesians 4:32.

83 *As Leon Morris describes . . . a loving person."* Leon Morris, *Luke* in the Tyndale New Testament Commentaries (Grand Rapids: Eerdmans, 1974), 129.

83 *"Christ says in effect . . . Martyn Lloyd-Jones.* David Martyn Lloyd-Jones, *Studies in the Sermon on the Mount*, vol. 1 (1971; rpt., Grand Rapids: Eerdmans, 1979), 305.

84 *"Repay no one . . . Paul commands.* Romans 12:17.

84 *Instead, "outdo . . . honor."* Romans 12:10.

84 *Elisabeth Elliot's . . . in Ecuador*. Read Elisabeth Elliot's story of evangelizing the Waorani people in *The Savage My Kinsman* (New York: Harper and Brothers, 1961).

84 *Bishop Handley . . . of his love."* H. C. G. Moule, *The Epistle to the Romans* (1928; rpt., Fort Washington: Christian Literature Crusade, 1975), 338.

84 *Come before the Lord's . . . your name's sake*. Owen Collins, ed., *Classic Christian Prayers* (New York: Testament Books, 2003), 55.

CHAPTER 10: THE CONFESSION PROMISE

86 *As Herbert . . . a till . . . ."* Herbert, 117.

87 *No one is . . . to the filth*. See Job 7:21; 9:2, 28-31; and 14:16-17.

87 *What he can't . . . by God*. See Job 6:30; 10:6-7; 16:17; 23:11-12; and 27:4-6.

87 *He is "in . . . friends may say*. See Job 9:15, 20.

87 *"It is the . . . from God."* Hartley, 421.

88 *Reverend Dimmesdale . . . rid themselves."* Nathaniel Hawthorne, *The Scarlet Letter* (New York: Signet, 1959), 230.

88 *"Secrets are . . . research*. Anita E. Kelly, *The Psychology of Secrets* (New York: Kluwer/Plenum, 2002), 9, 217.

89 *As Budziszewski* . . . was wrong." Budziszewski, 145 (italics his).

90 *I cannot . . . I am . . . ."* These lines are from Charles Wesley, "Jesus, Lover of My Soul."

90 *If you love . . . the psalmist*. Psalm 97:10.

90 *I am forever . . . it wants."* Romans 13:14b.

91 *David knew . . . hidden faults.*" Psalm 19:12; see also Moses' prayer in Psalm 90:8.

91 *Our Father . . . the west.*" Psalm 103:12.

91 *You may need . . . Jesus directed.* See Matthew 18:15-18; 5:23-24.

92 *As Richard Foster . . . to change.*" Foster, *Celebration of Discipline* (San Francisco: Harper and Row, 1978), 137.

93 *Eugene Peterson . . . can't love.*" Peterson, *Christ Plays*, 316.

93 *The one who . . . wise man.* Proverbs 28:13.

CHAPTER 11: THE STEWARDSHIP PROMISE

97 *To borrow . . . of its owner.* The novel is *Cry, The Beloved Country.*

97 *Cain's murder . . . for Cain.* Genesis 4:10.

97 *Covenant violation . . . Israel as well.* See Isaiah 5:6; 34:13; and Jeremiah 12:13, for example.

99 *"Listen to . . .* The Epic of Evolution." Ursula Goodenough, *The Sacred Depths of Nature* (New York: Oxford University Press, 1998), xvi.

99 *She calls it . . . natural beauty.*" Goodenough, xvi, xvii.

99 *Nature is . . . the divine.* Goodenough, 46.

99 *No' "creator . . . naturalism.* Goodenough, 171.

99-100 *Goodenough even . . . Living God.*" Goodenough, 13-14, 102.

100 *In fact . . . environmental hazard.*" Edward Wilson, *In Search of Nature* (Washington: Island Press, 1996), 186.

100 *He contends . . . of the earth.]*" Wilson, 184.

100 *You see . . . our environment.* Wilson, 184-5.

100 *The only "moral . . . Wilson claims.* Wilson, 175.

100-101 *Goodenough perceives . . . difficult as they are.* Goodenough, 139-40.

101 *God's "invisible . . . without excuse."* Romans 1:20.

101 *The main premise . . . your creatures."* Psalm 104:24.

101 *The "landscape . . . bring God glory.* Gerard Manley Hopkins, "Pied Beauty" in *The Literature of England*, vol. 2, 5th ed., eds. G. K. Anderson and W. E. Buckler (Glenview, IL: Scott, Foresman and Company, 1968), 1413.

102 *He promises . . . to this one.* See Isaiah 65 and Revelation 21-22.

102 *Until fulfillment . . . his holiness.* This is Paul's injunction in Ephesians 4:20–30 and Colossians 3:5–17.

CONCLUSION: THORNY CROWN, INTEGRITY'S CROWN

106 *He has "signed" . . . legal document.* Literally the Hebrew text says, "behold my *tau*." The *tau* is the last letter in the Hebrew alphabet and was shaped like an "X" or a cross in old script. We might think of it as our signature or making our "X" on the dotted line.

107 *He speaks of . . . bring reconciliation.* Job 9:33.

107 *"I have one . . . before God."* Job 16:19–21.

107 *This Redeemer . . . Job's defense.* Job 19:25–27.

107 *His mediator . . . with God.* Job 33:22–26.

107 *On His cross . . . legal demands.* Colossians 2:14.

108 *So what is . . . contains us.* Wendell Berry, *A Timbered Choir: The Sabbath Poems 1979-1997* (New York: Counterpoint, 1998), 215.